PORTRAIT OF JUNG

PORTRAIT OF JUNG

An Illustrated Biography

Gerhard Wehr

Translated by W. A. Hargreaves

HERDER AND HERDER

1971
HERDER AND HERDER NEW YORK
232 Madison Avenue, New York 10016

23456789 BPBP 798765432

Original edition: *C. G. Jung in Selbstzeugnissen und Bilddokumenten,* © 1969 by Rowohlt Taschenbuch Verlag GmbH, Reinbek bei Hamburg.

Library of Congress Catalog Card Number: 73-150141
English translation © 1971, by Herder and Herder, Inc.
Manufactured in the United States

CONTENTS

Carl Gustav Jung.

A TURNING POINT

IN the last few centuries human reason has constructed an astonishing image of man, the world, and reality. Everything that can be measured, counted, or weighed has been given a place in it. But any manifestation of consciousness below or above what is regarded as normal in "modern" man was treated with great skepticism and prejudice if not with downright rejection.

Just past the midpoint of what Martin Heidegger called the darkest yet of all the centuries of the modern era, in the year 1856, Sigmund Freud was born. As a psychiatrist, he was destined to use the patterns of thought of his times in order to penetrate by analytical methods into the depths of the human psyche, into the "unconscious" which until then had been little more than the object of conjecture. This discoverer was destined to unmask many things. The present generation has been slow to realize the debt of gratitude it owes him.

In Carl Gustav Jung, Freud found the disciple who could face him as a creative partner of equal standing and supply that constructive criticism which modern psychological research demanded. Who was Jung and what were his aims?

"I am a doctor who has to deal with the ills affecting man and his times and who is intent on finding remedies appropriate to the reality of the ailment. Psychopathological investigations have led me to resuscitate historical symbols and figures from the dust of their graves. I have seen that it is not enough to cure my patients of their symptoms . . .

"What we need is not so much ideals as a little wisdom and introspection, a careful religious consideration of the experiences coming from the unconscious. I say 'religious' deliberately because it seems to me that these experiences which help to make life healthier or more beautiful or more complete or more meaningful for oneself or one's loved ones justify the confession: it was divine mercy."[1] This personal testimony came from Carl Gustav Jung in old age during an interview he gave to Georg Gerster for the *Weltwoche*. It was also his answer to the open or implicit question as to whether C. G. Jung was speaking as an advocate of medieval mysticism or as an Oriental initiate, as a religious reformer or even as a founder of a modern religion. This question is pertinent since Jung did not confine himself to direct practice but let his mind range widely in order to examine the testimony of spiritual-religious experience, the traditional wisdom and the practices of Asia, as well as early Christian Gnosticism and the alchemy of the late Middle Ages.

Another elemant is worthy of consideration if one wishes to regard the explorer of the archetypes in the human psyche, that is, of the collective unconscious, not merely as a man who just describes and subsequently interprets the experiences of other epochs of consciousness.

Jung drew from his own sensitive experience. His late work *Memories, Dreams, Reflections,* recorded and edited by Aniela Jaffé, his pupil and collaborator, bears eloquent witness to the multi-layered medical-psychotherapeutic life work of Jung. Of those things which are revealed to him, that is, of his dreams and visions, he says: "These form the *prima materia* of my scientific work. They were the fiery magma out of which the stone that had to be

8

worked was crystallized."[2] And elsewhere he said that all his creative work originated in these visions.

Was he then really a mystic who followed that mysterious path leading inwards? That implication cannot be ignored. Anyone wishing to understand the research of this Swiss psychiatrist must try to apprehend the nature and effect of these "visions."

THE BEGINNINGS

Carl Gustav Jung was born on July 26, 1875, in the country parish of Kesswill on Lake Constance in the Swiss canton of Thurgau. He was the son of Johann Paul Achilles Jung (1842–1896), a minister of the Lutheran

Birthplace in Kesswill on Lake Constance.

Reformed Church, and his wife Emilie, née Preiswerk (1848–1923).

As we know from Aniela Jaffeé's inquiries, the Jung family came originally from Mainz. "Jung's great-grandfather, doctor Ignaz Jung (1759–1831), left Mainz to go to Mannheim. In the Napoleonic campaigns he was in charge of a military hospital. His brother, Sigismund von Jung (1745–1824), who was conferred the noble title 'von,' was the Bavarian Chancellor. He was married to Schleiermacher's youngest sister." Religion and medicine, faith and science, seem always to have played a part in the Jung family. There were also theologians on the mother's side, in the Preiswerk family. Carl Gustav Jung (1794–1864), the grandfather, a doctor, went to Switzerland when he was twenty-eight and took an active part in the expansion of the University of Basle. His grandson said of him: "He was a strong and striking personality, a great organizer, extremely active, sparkling, witty, and eloquent. I myself was still caught up in his wake. It was commonly said that Professor Jung was indeed a great man. His children were very much impressed by him."[3]

When Carl Gustav was about six months old, the minister's family went to spend four years in Laufen in the immediate vicinity of the Falls of the Rhine at Schaffhausen.

"My memories begin with my second or third year. I recall the vicarage, the garden, the laundry house, the church, the castle, the Falls, the small castle of Wörth, and the sexton's farm. These are nothing but islands of memory . . . "[4] These memories, especially those things which even in Carl Gustav's early childhood left unforgettable impressions, should be seen quite positively as inner experiences. Here without any doubt is the center of gravity of the biography. Introversion is what the psychol-

Parents: Pastor Johann Paul Achilles Jung and his wife Emilie, née Preiswerk, March, 1876.

ogist later, in his typology, called this condition in which the mind turns inwards upon itself; and at the age of eighty-three he remarked as he looked backwards: "In the end the only events in my life worth telling are those when the imperishable world irrupted into this transitory one. All other memories of travels, people and my surroundings have paled beside these interior happenings. Many people have participated in the story of our times and written about it; if the reader wants an account of that, let him turn to them or get somebody to tell it to him. Recollection of the outward events of my life has largely faded or disappeared. But my encounters with the 'other' reality, my bouts with the unconscious, are indelibly engraved upon my memory. In that realm there has always been wealth in abundance, and everything else has lost importance by comparison."[5]

The realm of dreams and visions was opening for Jung and it was to prove throughout his life a fount providing primary matter for his scientific work. Already significant was the first dream he remembered having, as a three- or four-year-old boy in Laufen. According to the contents of the dream which was to engage Jung's attention all his life—characteristically enough, he mentioned it for the first time at the ripe age of 65—the boy was confronted by a dark, rectangular wall lined with masonry. He found it in a large meadow not far from his parents' house. The following account is in the autobiographical notes:

"I ran forward curiously and peered down into it. Then I saw a stone stairway leading down. Hesitantly and fearfully I descended. At the bottom was a door with a round arch, closed off by a green curtain. It was a big, heavy curtain of worked stuff like brocade, and it looked very sumptuous. Curious to see what might be hidden behind, I pushed it aside. I saw before me in the dim light a

At the age of six, November 18, 1881.

rectangular chamber about thirty feet long. The ceiling was arched and of hewn stone. The floor was laid with flagstones, and in the center a red carpet ran from the entrance to a low platform. On this platform stood a wonderfully rich golden throne. I am not certain, but perhaps a red cushion lay on the seat. It was a magnificent throne, a real king's throne in a fairy tale. Something was standing on it which I thought at first was a tree trunk twelve to fifteen feet high and about one and a half to two feet thick. It was a huge thing, reaching almost to the ceiling. But it was of a curious composition: it was made of skin and naked flesh, and on top there was something like a rounded head with no face and no hair. On the very top of the head was a single eye, gazing motionlessly upwards . . . ''[6]

It was only many years later that the dreamer realized something of the significance of what he had seen, and only the experienced psychiatrist knew that the boy was confronted with the creative principle in the shape of the phallic archetype. "Through this childhood dream I was initiated into the secrets of the earth. . . . It was an initiation into the realm of darkness."[7]

These and similar happenings were the first of those spiritual experiences which continued into old age and repeatedly broke through that wall which "normally" stands between the rational and the irrational, the conscious and the unconscious, this world and the other scious and the unconscious, this world and the other sensibility and certainly fateful assumptions made this possible. Then there was a fall from a staircase, a serious head injury, and once he hovered between life and death; later, he had fainting spells from time to time. In his autobiography he even goes so far as to speak of a disagreeable resistance to life in this world. All this

14

strengthens the impression that this man seemed to be falling out of joint and that, because of it, he was all the more receptive to the images and figures of an inescapable shadow world.

This state of affairs must have given the boy his first fundamental problems to tackle. True, he lived the life of his schoolfellows. (In 1879 his father had taken up a post in the parish of Klein-Hüningen near Basle.) But the boy was leading a double life, so to speak. He thought he was actually two different persons, and living in two different periods. He was first of all a schoolboy in Basle obliged to work hard, especially at mathematics, gymnastics and drawing in order to cope with the work. But: "Besides [this] world there existed another realm, like a temple in which anyone who entered was transformed and suddenly overpowered by a vision of the whole cosmos, so that he could only marvel and admire, forgetful of himself. Here

Behind the parsonage in Klein-Hüningen near Basle.

lived the 'Other,' who knew God as a hidden, personal, and at the same time suprapersonal secret. Here nothing separated man from God; indeed, it was as though the human mind looked down upon Creation simultaneously with God." [8]

And so, in this way, personality 1 faced personality 2. Jung indicated that this play and counterplay of the two "persons" was in no way a split in the pathological sense. Personality 2 the inner man, which plays such an important part in the realm of religion, took precedence in his life as well, and he always endeavored to give full scope to anything coming from within him and claiming his attention.

This hidden side of his life represented even for the boy a secret condition in which he was scarcely understood by anybody with the possible exception of his mother. "My mother was a very good mother to me . . . and then her unconscious personality would suddenly put in an appearance. That personality was unexpectedly powerful: a somber, imposing figure possessed of unassailable authority—and no bones about it. I was sure that she consisted of two personalities, one innocuous and human, the other uncanny." [9]

With his father it was quite different. The son looked up to him respectfully as well but with unconcealed skepticism. Not only did the father not understand those things which moved the boy most deeply; he was not even aware of them, according to the descriptions of him in *Memories, Dreams, Reflections*. The theologian who performed the duties of his ministry with self-evident loyalty and whose tastes were chiefly philological knew absolutely nothing of an inner world of experience. Even as a boy, at the time when his father was giving him boring lessons to prepare him for confirmation, Carl Gustav Jung became convinced

16

that many theologians, including his father, had not the slightest religious experience of what they preached and endeavored to explain: "Suddenly I understood that God was, for me at least, one of the most certain and immediate of experiences." But this certainty was a lonely one. "My preoccupations with personality No. 2 were leading me in increasing measure to depressions. For everywhere in the realm of religious questions I encountered only locked doors, and if ever one door should chance to open I was disappointed by what lay behind it . . . I felt completely alone with my certainties. More than ever I wanted someone to talk with, but nowhere did I find a point of contact; on the contrary, I sensed in others an estrangement, a distrust, an apprehension which robbed me of speech. That, too, depressed me."[10] But it was not just while passing through the stage of adolescence that he felt he had been cast into an almost unbearable loneliness. Mystery dominated his whole life. It was certainly not simply as an expression of bitterness, but as a sober assessment of the capacity for understanding of the people around him, that Jung wrote at the age of eighty-three: "Today as then, I am a solitary, because I know things and must hint at things which other people do not know, and usually do not even want to know."[11]

We are reminded here of Faust's words, the poetic force of which poured into Jung's soul like some miraculous balsam and supplied him with an answer to his question about the nature of evil:

Can anyone speak out that name and live?
The few to whom the secret came in part,
Who foolishly indeed poured out their heart
And told the mob their inmost mystery,
Alas! were always crucified and burnt.

17

Jung never let it be doubted that great energy came from those experiences of his early life and made its mark on his later life and all his creative work. Emphatic proof of this is supplied by the detailed descriptions in *Memories, Dreams, Reflections*. What the psychiatrist could interpret only through a self-analysis lasting for decades and involving observation and research appeared gradually in the child's soul as he grew up: a world in which there were not only events taking place in space and time, but a reality— perhaps one ought to say a dimension of reality—which was reflected on the psychic plane as images, and was felt as something real by the observer in his dreams and in his imagining, which had the quality of waking dreams. Neither school nor church supplied that pastoral care the boy so needed. Not only did the school fail as an educative force but even the church itself in which his father ministered was found lacking: "Church gradually became a place of torment for me. For there men dared to preach aloud—I am tempted to say, shamelessly—about God, about His intentions and actions. There people were exhorted to have those feelings and to believe that secret which I knew to be the deepest, innermost certainty, a certainty not to be betrayed by a single word. I could only conclude that apparently no one knew about this secret, not even the parson, for otherwise no one would have dared to expose the mystery of God in public and to profane those inexpressible feelings with stale sentimentalities."[12]

And so, left alone with his thoughts and his suprasensual gift of perception, he had to look for his own way of finding answers to his questions. He was still going to school from Klein-Hüningen. At the age of eleven (1886) he began to attend the Gymnasium in Basle. Many of his schoolfellows were the sons of wealthy parents who could

With his parents and sister Gertrud, about 1893.

afford to give their children plenty of pocket-money and
send them on pleasant trips during vacations. Things were
different for Carl Gustav. "Then, for the first time, I
became aware how poor we were, that my father was a
poor country parson and I a still poorer parson's son who
had holes in his shoes and had to sit for six hours in school
with wet socks. I began to see my parents with different
eyes, and to understand their cares and worries. For my
father in particular I felt compassion—less, curiously
enough, for my mother. She always seemed to me the
stronger of the two."[13]

Between the ages of sixteen and seventeen this mood of
depression began to disappear. The young man was now

discovering the great world of ideas and reading about figures from the history of philosophy. ''I began systematically pursuing questions I had consciously framed . . . Above all I was attracted to the thought of Pythagoras, Heraclitus, Empedocles and Plato, despite the long-windedness of Socratic argumentation.''[14] Whereas the Aristotelian intellectualism of St. Thomas left him cold, Schopenhauer's philosophy was a great find: ''Schopenhauer's somber picture of the world had my undivided approval, but not his solution of the problem.''[15]

Side by side with these excursions in search of landmarks in philosophy, there were events which drove him out of his everyday life into God's boundless world. By God's world, however, Jung did not just mean a sphere of pure spirituality far removed from this world. He felt that the earth and, more especially, its flora were another form of this reality. ''This expression 'God's world' may sound sentimental to some ears. For me it did not have this character at all. To 'God's world' belonged everything suprahuman—dazzling light, the darkness of the abyss, the cold impassivity of infinite space and time, and the uncanny grotesqueness of the irrational world of chance. 'God,' for me, was everything—and anything but 'edifying.' ''[16]

The question of a choice of career arose. Science and both the historical and archaeological aspects of the Greco-Roman, Egyptian, and prehistoric epochs had awakened the interest of the schoolboy: ''What appealed to me in science were the concrete facts and their historical background, and in comparative religion the spiritual problems into which philosophy also entered. In science I missed the factor of meaning; and in religion, that of empiricism.'' It is interesting to note how his two personalities reacted to his inclinations towards a career: ''Science met, to a very large extent, the needs of No. 1

As a student in Basle (seated third from left), about 1896.

personality, whereas the humane or historical studies provided beneficial instruction for No. 2.''[17] Evidently theology did not figure in the list. Even his father almost advised against it. The son said quite plainly that it was theology or, to put it more plainly, ecclesiastical Christianity in general which had estranged the parson's son from his father. ''But I continued to waver between science and the humanities. Both powerfully attracted me.''[18]

If Jung once said that he had a strong feeling that he was influenced by things or questions which had been left unfinished or gone unanswered by his parents, grandparents, or ancestors, this fateful remark has to be considered along with other factors when examining the decision about a career. Particularly influential was his ancestor Carl Gustav Jung, who was professor of medicine at the University of Basle from 1822 to 1864 and made a

21

reputation for himself as anatomist, surgeon, obstetrician, and specialist in internal diseases. According to the portrait of Jung by Franz N. Riklin, this grandfather who had long since been dead played a decisive role—together with purely practical necessity—when Jung decided to take up the study of medicine. The liberal willfulness of this ancestor, combined with equally strong traits in the forbears on his mother's side, was alive in him too, and was probably the driving force in his aspiration to achieve something great on his own account.

Apart from the family's relatively modest circumstances, the death of the father in 1896 created a serious financial problem for him as a medical student at the University of Basle. Jung solved this problem by taking up the post of junior assistant and selling privately a small collection of antiques. Jung confesses: "I would not have missed this time of poverty. One learns to value simple things . . . Looking back, I can only say that my student days were a good time for me."[19]

At the end of the first year he added to the study of the compulsory subjects an acquaintance with spiritual literature such as it was at the end of the nineteenth century. "The observations of the spiritualists, weird and questionable as they seemed to me, were the first accounts I had seen of objective psychic phenomena. Names like Zoellner and Crookes impressed themselves on me, and I read virtually the whole of the literature available to me at the time."[20] Carl du Prel, Eschenmayer, Passavant, Justinus Görres, and seven volumes of Swedenborg provided him with his first theoretical and speculative basis. Spiritualistic and parapsychological experiments were carried out and the results recorded. Although Jung treated these experiments critically and skeptically, the observations he made during this time seemed to him to offer valuable material

22

Carl Gustav Jung (1794–1864), the paternal grandfather. Painting by
Beltz, 1848, in the old hall of the University of Basle.

for the dissertation he had to present for his medical
doctorate, which appeared in 1902 under the title of *The
Psychology and Pathology of Supposed Occult Phenomena.* "I
had discovered some objective facts about the human
psyche. Yet the nature of the experience was such that
once again I was unable to speak of it. I knew no one to
whom I could have told the whole story."[21]

When Jung was preparing for the state examination in
1900, he was still not at all clear in what direction his

future work as a doctor would lie. That it might be psychiatry did not seem to him to be very likely. But when he opened *The Textbook of Psychiatry* by Krafft-Ebing, He recognized the beginning of the path for which he had been looking for so long. In a London radio and television program on the occasion of his eightieth birthday, Jung emphasized once again the significance of this introduction to Krafft-Ebing: "And it caused me tremendous emotion then. I was quite overwhelmed by a sudden sort of intuitive understanding. I wouldn't have been able to formulate it clearly then, but I felt I had touched a focus. And then on the spot I made up my mind to become a psychiatrist, because there was a chance to unite my philosophical interest with natural science and medical science; that was my chief interest from then on."[22] Fate had presented him with a subject which could occupy him for the whole of his life, and the young doctor had accepted it.

In 1900, soon after the conclusion of his university studies, Jung entered the Psychiatric University Clinic of Burghölzli in Zurich in order to work as assistant under Eugen Bleuler, Professor of Psychiatry. At that time hypnosis was chiefly used in the treatment of mental illness. In the Burghölzli Clinic also, patients were treated by hypnosis with varying success. In the Eighties of the nineteenth century a young specialist in nervous disorders had gone expressly from Vienna to Paris and Nancy in order to study under leading authorities the various kinds of treatment associated with hypnosis. In 1895 the same doctor—it was Sigmund Freud—had published in collaboration with Josef Breuer his pioneering *Studies on Hysteria*. Freud's work, *The Interpretation of Dreams*, which opened a new chapter in psychiatric research and psychotherapeutic methods of treatment, appeared in 1900.

Eugen Bleuler.

Jung, who came across *The Interpretation of Dreams* in that very same year, had to wait six years before becoming more closely acquainted with Freud's rapidly increasing output of writing, and with the psychoanalytic school in Vienna that was gathering around him; later, too, was to come the exchange of ideas with the pioneer of modern depth psychology.

The following years at the Burghölzli Clinic saw Jung

With his wife Emma, née Rauschenbach, about 1903.

fully occupied with the routine work of a resident physician. But in addition he found time to finish his dissertation. He also wrote some studies on word association, a
method which had been employed before Jung. The test
subject is given a series of words and is requested to reply
to each of them by association. The time taken to react is
noted. During the course of these experiments "complexes tinged with feeling" emerged—later, the word
"complex" came to be used alone. The word signified the
contents of the personal unconscious that Jung distinguished from the "archetypes" which he discovered
later and which are the expression of the "collective
unconscious."

Jung made good progress with his studies. His colleagues recognized the quality of his work. Soon the
professional world was taking an interest in what was going
on at the Burghölzli Clinic. In 1905 Jung qualified as

1904.

academic lecturer and in addition took over the duties of
senior physician. But with all these notable successes Jung
did not forget that he had come to learn. "Burghölzli was
where I served my years of apprenticeship." He knew too
how much he really owed to the people who were
entrusted to him for treatment. "From my encounters
with patients and with the psychic phenomena which they
have paraded before me in an endless stream of images, I

have learned an enormous amount—not just knowledge, but above all insight into my own nature. And not the least of what I have learned has come from my errors and defeats. I have had mainly women patients who often entered into the work with extraordinary conscientiousness, understanding and intelligence. It was essentially because of them that I was able to strike out on new paths in therapy. A number of my patients became my disciples in the original sense of the word, and have carried my ideas out into the world. Among them I have made friendships that have endured decade after decade."[23]

THE MEETING AND BREAK
WITH FREUD

In July 1906 Jung wrote the preface to his *The Psychology of Dementia Praecox*, which appeared in print in 1907. At this time he began to exchange ideas in writing and also to make personal contact with Sigmund Freud. It is therefore instructive to read how Jung assessed the significance of Freud at the outset:

"Even a superficial glance at my work will show how much I am indebted to the brilliant discoveries of Freud . . . I can assure you that in the beginning I naturally entertained all the objections that are customarily made against Freud in the literature . . . Fairness to Freud, however, does not imply, as many fear, unqualified submission to a dogma; one can very well maintain an independent judgment." Jung went into the problems which Freud had tackled and continued: "If I, for instance, acknowledge the complex mechanisms of dreams and hysteria, this does not mean that I attribute to the infantile sexual trauma the exclusive importance that Freud apparently does. Still less does it mean that I place sexuality so predominantly in the foreground, or that I grant it the psychological universality which Freud, it seems, postulates in view of the admittedly enormous role which sexuality plays in the psyche . . . Nevertheless, all these things are the merest trifles compared with the psychological principles whose discovery is Freud's greatest merit; and to them the critics pay far too little attention."[24] (It is debatable whether Jung is not somewhat optimistic in his use of the word "trifles." For Freud, understanding of the libido as defined and practiced by him was at all events never a trifle.)

These remarks, which are the expression of Jung's positive views at a time when the psychological movement was still in its infancy, do not stand in isolation. Although certain distinct reservations cannot be overlooked, Jung's support for Freud's pioneering activity can hardly be overrated. Ernest Jones, the disciple and biographer of Freud, has written that in Vienna in those days prejudice against Freud was so great that it was difficult to find any disciple with a reputation to lose. The prejudice was made worse by the fact that Freud's first disciples were almost without exception Jews like himself. In view of the ever-increasing anti-Semitism, he must have been particularly worried lest the cause of psychoanalysis should come to be misunderstood as an exclusively Jewish concern. Nor did the professional world outside Vienna show very much understanding; Freud was at first completely rejected by large numbers of his colleagues, some of whom were downright suspicious. As late as 1910, a medical Privy Councillor by the name of Weygandt thought it his business to declare during a discussion at a medical

Sigmund Freud.

congress in Hamburg that Freud's theories were no concern of science but were rather a matter for the police . . .

In *The Psychology of the Unconscious*, published in 1917, Jung mentions the response to Freud's most fundamental works: "The first work of any magnitude (Freud-Breuer: *Studies on Hysteria*, 1895) in this field awakened only the faintest echo, in spite of the fact that it introduced an entirely new conception of the neuroses. A few writers spoke of it appreciatively and then, on the next page, proceeded to explain their hysterical cases in the same old way . . . Freud's next publications remained absolutely unnoticed, although they put forward observations which were of incalculable importance for psychiatry. When, in the year 1900, Freud wrote the first real psychology of dreams (a veritable Stygian darkness had hitherto reigned over this field), people began to laugh, and when he actually began to throw light on the psychology of sexuality in 1905 (*Drei Abhandlungen zur Sexualtheorie*, 1905; trans. by A. A. Brill as *Three Contributions to the Sexual Theory*, New York, 1930), laughter turned to insult.''[25] This attitude was slow to change, especially as child psychologists were also active in withholding due recognition from Freud—for example, by delaying for a considerable period his appointment to a professorial chair. It was by the devious way of stigmatization that Freud secured the publicity still accorded his name and work. At the age of thirty-one, Jung was taking a considerable risk in declaring his support for Freud. The young head-physician at the Burghölzli Clinic in Zurich could conceivably have lost his scientific reputation round about the year 1906.

In February 1907, in response to an invitation from Freud, the first meeting took place in Vienna at 19 Bergstrasse where Freud lived until he was expelled in 1938. Jung's purpose was to delineate for himself the Austrian's distinctive mentality and to determine whether the lines of demarcation he had perceived did in fact exist. Jung recorded that they met at one o'clock in the afternoon and spoke for thirteen hours almost without a break. He also confessed that Freud at first seemed to him to be a somewhat strange person, as he seemed to so many

31

other contemporaries. It is likely that the special atmosphere of the Vienna of the last decades of the old Austro-Hungarian Empire, as represented by a member of the Jewish intelligentsia, had a marked effect on a Swiss doctor shaped by quite different cultural traditions. Added to these environmental differences were their contrasting natures, about which Jung later said that, according to his typology, he described himself as an introvert, whereas Freud was a decided extravert (see below).

The differences between the two men showed up chiefly in factual and scientific matters. There was first of all Freud's sexual theory: "What he said about his sexual theory impressed me. Nevertheless, his words could not remove my hesitations and doubts. I tried to advance these reservations of mine on several occasions, but each time he would attribute them to my lack of experience. (Freud was fifty-one and Jung thirty-two.) Freud was right; in those days I had not enough experience to support my objections."[26] For the time being, Jung could only recognize how enormously important Freud's sexual theory was to him, both personally and philosophically. "Above all, Freud's attitude towards the spirit seemed to me highly questionable. Wherever, in a person or in a work of art, an expression of spirituality (in the intellectual, not the supernatural sense) came to light, he suspected it, and insinuated that it was repressed sexuality. Anything that could not be directly interpreted as sexuality he referred to as 'psychosexuality.'"[27] As is well known, Freud drew corresponding conclusions in his explanation of the roots and nature of culture when he asserted that culture was built on a renunciation of the sexual urge.

Jung did not conceal the strong impression that Freud had once made on him. "Freud was the first man of real importance I had encountered; in my experience up to

32

that time, no one else could compare with him. There was nothing the least trivial in his attitude. I found him extremely intelligent, shrewd, and altogether remarkable. And yet my first impressions of him remained somewhat tangled; I could not make him out."[28]

As for the meeting, there was obviously a combination of two elements: on the one side there was the generous recognition of the professional competence, indeed, of the brilliance of the Viennese psychiatrist and his greatness as a human being; on the other side, considerable differences were apparent. These differences were due in part to the dissimilarity of types and in part to a difference in intellectual approach. Freud, who was born in 1856 and was thus nineteen years older, was too much influenced in his thinking by the assumptions of his century. The science of that period made Freud give to the hypotheses he used as aids a dogmatic or doctrinal quality, and at a stage of uncertainty in his development he made no attempt to overcome those self-imposed limits to cognition. The words which the Berlin physiologist Emil Du Bois-Reymond spoke in 1872 and which then became famous: *"Ignoramus et ignorabimus"*—"We don't know and we shall never know"—express an attitude which was in some way akin to that of Freud. And then there was the skepticism tinged with materialism with which Freud turned so resolutely against the "black tide of mud of occultism" as he expressed himself in one of the first conversations with Jung. Freud thought he could strengthen the position he had taken with a "bulwark," namely, his idea of the libido. And so, when discussing this—it was about 1910—Freud said: "My dear Jung, promise me never to abandon the sexual theory. That is the most essential thing of all. You see, we must make a dogma of it, an unshakable bulwark." And Jung adds the comment:

33

"This was the thing that struck at the heart of our friendship. I knew that I would never be able to accept such an attitude."[29] Jung was certainly right when he pointed out that a dogma was an undisputable matter and had nothing to do with scientific judgment.

But what did Freud mean by occultism? It is no secret that genuine esoterism had fallen into discredit because of so much obscurity and extravagance. A glance at the relevant literature dating from the turn of the century will fully confirm this. But Jung surmises: "What Freud seemed to mean by 'occultism' was virtually everything that philosophy and religion, including the rising contemporary science of parapsychology, had learned about the psyche. To me the sexual theory was just as occult, that is to say, just as unproven a hypothesis, as many other speculative views. As I saw it, a scientific truth was a hypothesis which might be adequate for the moment but was not to be preserved as an article of faith for all time."[30]

For Jung the question as to whether and how far parapsychological phenomena and investigation of them can achieve an adequate refutation of the materialistic way of reasoning always had very great significance. But Freud rejected at that period around 1909 "this entire complex of questions as nonsensical, and did so in terms of so shallow a positivism that I had difficulty in checking the sharp retort on the tip of my tongue."[31] It was only several years later that Freud could bring himself to acknowledge that in this field of activity there was a real core of facts that had not yet been discovered and which he himself sought to get at by the analysis of dreams.

Jung describes an incident which took place at this time during a visit to Freud's apartment as follows: "While Freud was going on in this way [arguing against parapsychology being taken seriously], I had a curious sensation. It was as if my diaphragm were made of iron and were becoming red-hot—a glowing vault. And at that moment there was such a loud report in the bookcase, which stood right next to us, that we both started up in alarm, fearing the thing was going to topple over on us. I said to Freud: 'There, that is an example of a so-called exteriorization phenomenon.'—'Oh come,' he exclaimed. 'That is sheer bosh.'—'It is not,' I replied. 'You are mistaken, Herr Professor. And to prove my point of view I now predict that in a moment there will be another loud report!' Sure enough, no sooner had I said the words than the same detonation went off in the bookcase.''[32]

Jung had the impression that this incident aroused Freud's mistrust of him, and he had the feeling of having done something against him.

In fact, the incident was never discussed again. But in the Appendix to *Memories, Dreams, Reflections*, there is a letter from Sigmund Freud to Jung dated April 16, 1909, in which the subject of the poltergeist (as Freud calls it) is taken up again. This event occurred on the evening in which Freud formally adopted Jung as his eldest son and anointed him as his successor and crown prince—*in partibus infidelium*—and in which Jung divested Freud of his paternal dignity. Freud adds that the divesting seems to have given Jung as much pleasure as investing Jung's person gave Freud. To anoint Jung as his successor, to adopt him as his son and even as his eldest son, is confirmation of the high esteem in which the Viennese master held the young Swiss doctor, preferring him to his Viennese disciples.

Informative too is another passage in the same letter in which Freud conjures up (on a note of self-irony) this imaginary relationship of father and son: "I therefore don

Congress for Psychoanalysis, Weimar, 1911.

once more my horn-rimmed paternal spectacles and warn my dear son to keep a cool head and rather not understand something than make such great sacrifices for the sake of understanding. I also shake my wise grey locks over the question of psychosynthesis and think: well, that is how the young folks are; they really enjoy things only when they need not drag us along with them, where with our short breath and weary legs we cannot follow.''

But what was Jung's reaction to such hints? Jung states in his autobiographical *Memories*: ''I found our relationship exceedingly valuable. I regarded Freud as an older, more mature and experienced personality, and felt like a son in that respect.''[33] On the other hand, E. A. Bennet, an English friend and colleague of Jung, was clearly authorized to point out that none of the usual relationships of master and disciple had ever existed between Freud and Jung. At any rate, they were good colleagues. This was emphasized again in 1909 when both had been invited to deliver lectures at Clark University in Worcester, Massachusetts. This trip to America, on which they were accompanied by Ferenczi, one of Freud's disciples, lasted seven weeks, and they were together every day.

Jung returned from this trip not only with the distinction of an honorary doctorate of law, but with the knowledge that the genius of Freud seen by Jung in the sign of a father-projection placed personal authority above truth. This emerged from conversations with Freud about questions arising from the analysis of dreams. There is an account of them in Jung's *Memories, Dreams, Reflections.*

What actually led to the break? This question cannot be answered in one sentence; several factors were instrumental. But it would not be wrong to say that the meeting was only an episode—significant though it was—in the lives of the two personalities. Jung esteemed Freud highly and recognized that the results of his research were unique, but their acquaintanceship was, especially for him, a kind of transition. Lifelong collaboration was out of the question because of the differences in the premises from which the two men worked. Jung reached the conclusion that "Freud himself had a neurosis, no doubt diagnosable and one with highly troublesome symptoms, as I had discovered on our voyage to America." And then comes the observation: "Apparently neither Freud nor his disciples could understand what it meant for the theory and practice of psychoanalysis if not even the master could deal with his own neurosis." The absolute priority given to the psychoanalytical method and its identification with Freudian theory made Jung decide to put an end to collaboration: "There remained no choice for me but to withdraw."[34]

This "retreat" was marked by an advance in the literary field. Jung published his book *Wandlungen und Symbole der Libido* (Transformations and Symbols of the Libido), in which he took a subject central to Freud's doctrine—the definition of psychic energy—and gave it a new definition, one which was in opposition to Freud: "When I was working on my book about the libido and approaching the end of the chapter "The Sacrifice," I knew in advance that its publication would cost me my friendship with Freud." The question of incest is dealt with here, and this was a point which would inevitably bring out the dissimilarities in their fundamental views. The disagreement can also be illustrated by their different conceptions of a symbol. Freud's "symbols" can best be explained causally and have therefore the character of symptoms. In contrast to the symbolic archetypal aspect in Jung's interpretation, there is in Freud a personal and concrete interpretation of what is called a symbol. When by symbol Jung means an expression which refers to some fact that cannot be directly expressed, Freud confuses this reference with the fact itself. Jung cites as example the problem of incest and writes: "To me incest signifies a personal complication only in the rarest cases. Usually incest has a highly religious aspect, for which reason the incest theme plays a decisive part in almost all cosmogonies and in numerous myths. But Freud clung to the literal interpretation of it and could not grasp the spiritual significance of incest as a symbol."[35]

This statement by Jung, which is confirmed so plainly in the title of the book *Transformations and Symbols of the Libido*, could not be accepted by Freud without the surrender of his premises, the foundations of his psychoanalytical theory.

Jung has recorded in his autobiographical notes how deep and lasting was the effect of the break: "For two months I was unable to touch my pen, so tormented was I by the conflict. Should I keep my thoughts to myself, or should I risk the loss of so important a friendship?"[36] He took the risk and Freud broke with him. That was not all. Almost all Jung's friends for their part broke with him. But he had known that everything was at stake and that he had to stand up for his convictions.

C. G. Jung did not conclude his revealing chapter on Sigmund Freud without paying tribute to his erstwhile paternal friend and academic opponent. This he did on the occasion of Freud's death in 1939 when, in the *Baseler Nachrichten*, he praised Freud's psychoanalysis as an epoch-making work, saying that it represented the boldest attempt to master the riddles of the unconscious psyche on the seemingly solid ground of empiricism. "For us, then young psychiatrists, it was a source of illumination, while for our older colleagues it was an object of mockery."[37]

And the octogenarian added: "Freud's greatest achievement probably consisted in taking neurotic patients seriously and entering into their peculiar individual psychology . . . He saw with the patient's eyes, so to speak . . . He did not falter in the face of the unpopularity such an enterprise entailed. The impetus which he gave to our civilization sprang from his discovery of an avenue to the unconscious. By evaluating dreams as the most important source of information concerning the unconscious processes, he gave back to mankind a tool that had seemed irretrievably lost."[38]

How, for his part, did Freud feel about the departure of Jung after experiencing the loss of other friends as well from the Viennese circle of collaborators, for example, Adler and Stekel? When asked about the break, Freud told E. A. Bennet in 1932: "Jung was a great loss."

ELEMENTS OF A DOCTRINE

It is quite a formidable task to convey some impression of a doctrine possessing the volume, the profundity, and the range of subject matter which is to be found in the work of C. G. Jung. No author can do justice even by the authentic reproduction of definitions and descriptions by Jung himself. Any close follower of Jung's work knows how things have grown and continue to grow. "Elements of a Doctrine" can be put together, then, only with the greatest reserve.

Before Jung worked out the theoretical foundations from which special pronouncements about psychic facts or hypotheses could subsequently be made, Sigmund Freud had developed his ideas about the psyche—he uses the term "psychical apparatus." When studying the individual development of human beings, Freud came upon an extremely primitive level of the psyche which he called the "id." He asserted that it contained everything that we inherited, that was present at birth, that was fixed in the constitution—above all, therefore, the instincts which originate in their somatic organization and which find their first mental expression in the id in forms unknown to us. This id, according to Freud, is, as it were, surrounded by a cortical layer provided with organs for receiving stimuli and with apparatus for protection against too great stimulation. To this region he gave the name "ego." In addition to what is happening in the id province of the psyche, during the period of childhood and under the influence of upbringing, tradition, and environment, there is formed a kind of controlling agency known as the "superego." This structure, which might at first glance appear static, is dominated by forces which are located and active behind the tensions caused by the needs of the id. These id forces appear as instincts. They represent the body's demands on mental life. As is well known, Freud considered the energy of the instincts seeking this outlet—the "libido"—to be primarily based on sex, although at one period he thought that energy could come from a "death" instinct as well. On the basis of this theory, which accorded a place to the conscious and the unconscious, which recommended dreams or the analysis of dreams as the royal road to the images in the unconscious, and which made the development of psychopathology possible, Sigmund Freud erected his system of psychoanalysis. But it should be noted that a path of development can be traced leading from the mesmerism of the late eighteenth century to Freud's psychoanalysis at the turn of our century.

If one looks at the work and the method of Jung, one can see here too, of course, that the formation of hypotheses plays a due role in this new territory. But, without seeking to invent yet another contrast to Freud, we must respect Jung's point that he wanted to follow chiefly the empirical path, although the speculative element did occasionally have significance in supplying guidance. But with Jung, this element too was integrated into the empirical approach. Whatever reached him in the shape of a dream, or came—as he calls it—"intuitively," he always subjected to critical examination. It had to be shown in every case whether and how new insights could be linked with experiences already gained and confirmed. What Jung propounded as a heuristic hypothesis ought not therefore to be misinterpreted as something which was given once and for all, nor as a brick in a completed system, nor even as a dogma with a scientific trimming. Jung considered his views themselves as proposals and attempts to formulate a new, scientific psychology based primarily on direct experience with people.[39] "I have neither put forward a system nor a general theory but only formulated concepts to help me as tools, as is usually done in science."[40] *The British Medical Journal* therefore confirmed in 1952: "Facts first and theories later is the keynote of Jung's work. He is an empiricist first and last."[41]

As an empiricist Jung wishes to be a psychologist and a psychiatrist, to investigate and cure souls. Looked at from this perspective, what is the soul?

In 1939 Jung gave to an omnibus volume of essays by some of his disciples the title *Reality of the Soul,* and thus expressed the fundamental thesis which determines all his work: the soul is real. He pointed out that every experience is psychic. Everything felt by the senses, the whole

42

Oedipus and the Sphinx. Attic bowl from the fifth century B.C. Etruscan Museum, Vatican.

world which comes flooding in through the senses, can only be experienced through the images by means of which the objects of this world can be reflected. Hence the psyche is the essence of all reality, especially because it does not limit itself to the world without, which is converted into psychic images, but embraces above and beyond this the vast realm of psychic space within. And so Jung wrote in the above-mentioned book that the psyche is the most real essence because it alone has immediacy.

The psychologist can refer to psychic reality.[42] This reality presents itself in tremendous diversity, which is indicated by the fact that, according to Jung, all conceivable statements are the product of the human psyche. Hence there is a limitation to experience; this limitation coincides with the limits of the psyche beyond which we can see nothing. In all he wrote he stressed the point that he wished to keep strictly within the confines of his own subject: "I have never been inclined to think that our senses were capable of perceiving all forms of being . . . All comprehension and all that is comprehended is in itself psychic, and to that extent we are hopelessly cooped up in an exclusively psychic world."[43]

Within these boundaries, two realms can be established in the psyche: one is the realm which is called "consciousness," a realm in which one has complete "presence of mind," but in which variations in consciousness are possible. The other is the "unconscious," usually removed from the grip of the conscious. Jung explains: "The unconscious is not simply the unknown, it is rather the unknown psychic, and this we define on the one hand as all those things in us which, if they came to consciousness, would presumably differ in no respect from the known psychic contents, with the addition, on the other hand, of the psychoid system, of which nothing is known directly." Jung adds to this definition: "Everything of which I know, but of which I am not at the moment thinking; everything of which I was conscious but have now forgotten; everything perceived by my senses, but not noted by my conscious mind; everything which, involuntarily and without paying attention to it, I feel, think, remember, want, and do; all the future things that are taking shape in me and will sometime come to consciousness: all this is the content of the unconscious."[44]

In order to express the dynamic by which the psyche and what happens inside it are characterized, Freud had already chosen the word "libido." Jung adopted the term; however, he did not define it as sexual energy, but understood it as meaning "psychic energy" in general. Although he appropriated this idea of energy, Jung rejected a one-sided mechanistic conception of psychic happenings according to which they could always be understood causally. As he understood it, "the idea of energy is not that of a substance moved in space; it is a concept abstracted from relations of movement."[45] This was in 1928, and he continued: "Psychic energy appears, when actual, in the specific, dynamic phenomena of the psyche, such as instinct, wishing, willing, affect, attention, capacity for work, etc., which makes up the psychic forces. When potential, energy shows itself in specific achievements, possibilities, aptitudes, etc., which are its various states."[46]

In *Über die Energetik der Seele (On Psychic Energy)*, published in 1928, he set out all the connections in detail. For example, the most important phenomena possessing energy ("progression" and "regression" of the psyche) are explained, that is to say, we read how the libido "moves."

The dynamic of the libido is also, and not least, confirmed by observations made by Freud according to which psychic energy can be transferred from one object to another. This happens when the impulse energy in the object of an instinct is changed to a similar object. Religion and culture especially afford an abundance of interesting material in the shape of magic or symbolic actions. One only needs to think how closely related are sexuality and cultural activity in the life of primitive tribes in agriculture, fishing, hunting, war, and so on. The object in each case is to gather psychic energy in magical preliminary actions, such as dances and manipulations, and

Prometheus.

subsequently to concentrate it on the particular task
envisaged. This is the place for the symbolic gesture, the
symbolic action, the symbol as Jung understood it. These
symbols serve the purpose, among others, of directing
libido towards that which is represented symbolically. For
example, the purpose of fertility magic in the yearly
cultivation of crops is to make fruitful the earth, considered as the mother's womb, and to do that through the
symbolic happening.

A very important, presumably the decisive, discovery
made by Jung, and one which has since been linked with
his name, is that of the supra-individual conscious. True,
Sigmund Freud already recognized the existence of an

archaic and mythological way of thinking, but to Jung belongs the undeniable merit of having been the first to recognize this as a realm of the psyche, which is not limited to the individual but possesses "collective" characteristics. It was as the discoverer of the "collective unconscious" that Jung took the most significant step beyond Freud.

"A partly superficial layer of the unconscious is undoubtedly personal. We call it the personal unconscious. But this rests upon a deeper layer which no longer derives from personal experience or acquired knowledge, but is innate. This deeper layer is the so-called collective unconscious."[47] Jung has chosen this expression in order to stress the general nature of this psychic layer. We are dealing with an unconscious participation of the psyche in a rich treasure of images and symbols by which the individual human being is joined to humanity in general. And this is by no means a mere hypothesis, for as a practicing psychiatrist Jung observed how primitive and archaic symbols appeared in his patients. He noticed, for example, how occasionally in dreams an archaic God-image was manifested which was completely different from God as the patient conceived him in his waking consciousness. The assumption of a layer of the unconscious extending beyond the individual psyche was thus abundantly confirmed. In this connection Jung encountered a startling parallel between the accounts of healthy and ailing persons on the one hand and mythological or symbolic image formations on the other.

As a name for the collective unconscious stored in the psyche which would express its characteristic basic form, Jung chose the concept "archetype." He gave the following definition: "The archetype represents essentially an unconscious content which is changed when it becomes

47

The sun as the image of God. From R. Fludd, *Utriusque cosmi maioris scilicet et minoris metaphysica, physica atque technica et historia* (Oppenheim, 1617).

conscious and is perceived, and this change varies with the particular individual consciousness in which it appears."[48] And, for the sake of precision, Jung added in a footnote: "It is necessary, in order to be exact, to distinguish between 'archetype' and 'archetypal notions.' The archetype is a hypothetical form like that which is known in biology as a 'pattern of behavior.'" Thus it would be quite in Jung's sense to say that the archetypes which remain invisible give rise to archetypal mental images which enter the realm of human observation. Archetypes are the necessary postulates for these mental images. According to his definition, "archetypes" are "factors and motives which arrange psychic elements into certain (known as archetypal) images, the nature of which can only be recognized from the effect. They exist in the pre-conscious, and presumably it is they which form the structure dominants of the psyche."[49] Whereas the archetype itself remains unrecognizable in the unconscious, the archetypal image of any person under consideration is recognizable. The ego emerges from the flood of the individual and collective conscious. As a part of the psyche it is the center of the field of consciousness and above all its subject. When Jung speaks of the ego-complex, he means a complex of mental images connected with this center of consciousness.

Clearly distinguished from the ego is the self, which unites into a whole the complete psyche, the conscious and the unconscious. "As an empirical concept, the self designates the whole circumference which embraces all the psychic phenomena in man. It expresses the unity and wholeness of the total personality. But, insofar as the latter, because of its unconscious part, can be only partly conscious, the concept of the self is actually in part potentially empirical and therefore to this extent a postulate. In other words, it embraces what can be experienced and what cannot or what has not yet been experienced."[50] Jung shows us the archetypal character of this self which can assume, in dreams, myths, and fairy tales, the shape of personalities such as the leader, hero, or saviour, or represent itself in symbols of totality such as a circle, a square, a cross, and so on. "The self is not only the center but that circumference which embraces both consciousness and the unconscious; it is the center of this totality just as the ego is the center of the conscious mind." Thus the self is a magnitude placed above the conscious ego.

But how does the self attain totality? Jung's answer refers us to a process of psychic development which he calls "individuation." "Individuation means becoming a

49

Anthropos as *anima mundi* containing the four elements. From the *Philosophia Naturalis* of Albertus Magnus (Basle, 1560).

single, homogeneous being, and, insofar as 'individuality' embraces our innermost, last, and incomparable uniqueness, it also implies becoming one's own self. We could therefore translate individuation as 'coming to selfhood' or 'self-realization.' '''[51] The purpose of this psychic process of development which, in Jung's experience, relatively few people consciously pass through is to liberate the self from the false covering of the persona, that is to say, of the mask-like collective psyche which only gives the illusion of something individual, and, on the other hand, to free it from the suggestive force of unconscious images. Jung also speaks of the integration of the contents of the psyche which are capable of consciousness, as a result of which the ego-consciousness does not become identified with the self, although certain consequences for the ego-consciousness, which are just as remarkable as they are difficult to describe, are mentioned.[52] Jung also described this significant process as follows: "Individuation is in general the process whereby single persons are formed and assert their special nature and is especially the development of the psychological individual as a person different from the generality, from collective psychology. Individuation is therefore a process of differentiation having for its goal the development of the individual personality. The need for individuation is natural insofar as hindering individuation by a predominant or even exclusive compliance with collective standards signifies injury to the individual's vital activity."[53]

The analyst belonging to the school of Jung learns in his practice that the process of individuation into which a person might be drawn in the second half of his life may be felt as a very difficult and dangerous path. He sees himself confronted by everything which the unconscious has to offer in the shape of images, notions, dreams, and ideas. Archetypal figures flood up, so to speak, from the depths of the soul which otherwise remain unconscious. No man may embark on this adventure unprepared or without a guide. Esoteric thought has long been familiar with threshold experience of this nature. One endeavors by the appropriate training—in the East, for example, through the companionship and support of a guru, to fit oneself for the "encounter with the self." "Although everything is chiefly experienced in images, that is to say, symbolically, these are by no means merely imagined dangers but very real risks which may under certain circumstances involve a person's life. The chief danger lies in succumbing to the fascinating influence of the archetypes, which can most easily happen if one does not bring the archetypal images into one's consciousness. If a psychotic predisposition is present, it may in certain cases happen that the archetypal

51

figures, which possess a certain autonomy by virtue of their numinosity, will free themselves entirely from the control of consciousness and obtain complete independence, that is to say, they will produce the phenomena of madness."[54]

But how can a person involved in the process of individuation find his way?—Apart from the fact that a psychiatrist is required here, a special feature of the method of depth psychology as used by Jung calls for mention. It is the use of "amplification." By this is meant the widening and deepening of the experience, let us say, of the dream by similar or analogous images taken from the history of religion, culture, and ideas belonging to all epochs of humanity. Jolande Jacobi explains: "In Jung's amplification method, the single dream motives are enriched by an analogous material, related in sense, taken from pictures, symbols, myths, and so forth and are thus exhibited in all their possible nuances of meaning and in their various aspects until their significance appears with absolute clarity. Every single element of meaning thus determined is then connected with the next until the whole chain of dream motives is cleared up and ultimately verified through its own coherence."[55] It was then the duty of the doctor in conversation to make the patient familiar with the contents of these images and to guide and advise him during a course of treatment consisting of several stages.

It was possible for Jung to use this method of amplification in so masterly a fashion only because of his thorough research into the mythologies of the ancient cultures and the history of the ideas of East and West. Jung not only acquired a comprehensive knowledge of the Asiatic spiritual outlook, proof of which is to be found, for example, in his forewords and commentaries on fundamental works such as those of the Chinese esoteric tradition. He took a special look at the Gnostics of the first centuries A.D., at the medieval mystics and, last but not least, at the late medieval alchemists and Rosicrucians, and he collected and worked through their writings, which were sometimes very difficult to get hold of. Such important works by Jung as *Symbole der Wandlung* (*Symbols of Transformation*), *Psychologie der Alchemie* (*Psychology and Alchemy*), *Aion, Symbolik des Geistes* (*Symbols of the Mind*), *Mysterium Coniunctionis*, with their copious illustrations, could otherwise not have been written. They are also a very rich source of information for those who are less interested in the psychological-therapeutic approach of their author. Especially in the texts and illustrated documents of the alchemists there are important disclosures and parallels for psychic cesses, for instance, on the path of individuation.

Jung was able to widen his psychiatric-psychotherapeutic and literary studies in the area of his research by journeys to North Africa, Kenya and Uganda, to the American Pueblo Indians, and to India. It is significant that Jung penetrated into the sphere of these alien cultural circles in order to obtain knowledge on the spot from his own experience, but that he never sought to deny that he was rooted in the European and Christian world of ideas. He did indeed say once of his journeys to Africa: "It was as if I were this moment returning to the land of my youth, and as if I knew that dark-skinned man who had been waiting for me for five thousand years."[56] But in his account of his journey to India he wrote of the need to cherish the ancient European stock of ideas while he was absorbing impressions of an alien culture. By the way, Jung had things to say in his *Memories* about the relationship of Christ and Buddha which are worth consideration.

A very important element in Jung's theory which admittedly plays some part in other psychoanalytical sys-

1912.

tems in a different form, is the uncovering of the problem of opposites and the endeavor of the psychotherapist to achieve integration of opposites within a greater wholeness. In Jung we meet this state of affairs in a multiplicity of aspects. His thinking expresses itself in positions of absolute opposites and pursues the tension relationship existing between the opposite poles into the ethical consequence (for example, in the conflict situation). Opposites of this kind are, for example, the conscious and the unconscious, introversion and extraversion as an expression of the two possible basic attitudes of the psyche to the world around it; of the animus in woman and the anima in man we shall have something to say later. In *Versuch einer psychologischen Deutung des Trinitätsdogmas* (1948) (ET *A Psychological Approach to the Dogma of the Trinity*, 1942/ 1948), based on an Eranos lecture, Jung stated: "Life, being an energic process, needs opposites, for without opposition there is, as we know, no energy." This throws light on Jung's conception of psychic energy. The premises underlying this understanding lead to inferences which extend to the highest or deepest objects of faith and religious cognition. Jung continued: "The tension of opposites that makes energy possible is a universal law, fittingly expressed in the *yang* and *yin* of Chinese philosophy."[57] Because of these conceptions of energy, Jung interprets "God" not only as the essence of spiritual light, "appearing as the latest flower on the tree of evolution" and not only as the spiritual goal of salvation "in which all creation culminates," and not only as the essence of all striving to a goal and of perfection of all being. For him God is simultaneously "also the darkest, nethermost cause of Nature's blackest deeps," a notion which touches upon a "tremendous paradox which obviously reflects a profound psychological truth."[58]

What Jung said in 1928 in the essay *On Psychic Energy*

The alchemistic quaternity: the Three and the One. From the *Rosarium Philosophorum* (Frankfurt, 1550).

was enlarged upon in later works such as *A Psychological Approach to the Dogma of the Trinity,* in which he expresses ideas about abolishing the Christian formula of the Trinity in favor of a divine quaternity in which the devil as an autonomous and eternal member of the Godhead and as the adversary of Christ would complete the divine Trinity: "As the adversary of Christ, he [the devil] would have to take up an equivalent counterposition and be, like him, a 'son of God.' But that would lead straight back to certain Gnostic views according to which the devil, as Satanaël, is God's first son, Christ being the second."[59] Riwkah Schärf, a disciple of Jung, has traced the figure of Satan in the Old Testament in a remarkable study.[60]

So we see that Jung encountered the problem of

divine. And thus his pronouncements refer to themes which are central to divinity and Christian theology, although it must be said that they are far from being part of the doctrine of the orthodox church which is obliged to reject them as heretical speculations. Because of his knowledge of the history of religion, Jung knew only too well that in this question of the problem of opposites he was dealing with Gnostic-heretical ideas. It must of course be understood that the use of the word "heretical" in this context does not imply any value judgment.

On the other hand, we must also bear in mind that Jung was not concerned with metaphysical pronouncements. He remained a psychologist even when his gaze was directed at objects which belong to the competence of theologians or philosophers of religion. What made Jung deal also with these subjects was his interest in the psychic element, which of course had been neglected by scholars in other disciplines. So the psychologist was not guilty of metabasis, of illegitimately deserting his own field of competence; he remained a psychologist even when he considered realities of the spiritual and divine or religious world in their significance for the human psyche. Finally, Jung could argue that the religious conceptions, even the dogmas of the Christian Church for which he showed the greatest respect, came into being after the psyche had reflected and actively shaped them. "In itself any scientific theory, no matter how subtle, has, I think, less value from the standpoint of psychological truth than religious dogma, for the simple reason that a theory is necessarily highly abstract and exclusively rational, whereas dogma expresses an irrational whole by means of imagery."[61] The quotation is taken from *Psychology and Religion* (1940), which contains the Terry Lectures delivered at Yale University in 1937. What Jung said here and in a similar

57

connection about the formulation of religious revelation has not yet been taken sufficiently seriously and discussed by theology. It would be a dangerous and false conclusion—and Jung warns theologians about this—if the attempt were to be made to confuse the "image of God" in man with the reality of God and to take this image of God which the psychologist sees shining in the psyche as a proof for or against this reality.

Whereas the subject of religion and psychology leads straight into the heights and depths of Jung's psychology, the two concepts which we have already mentioned, "animus" and "anima," belong to the elements of the doctrine. Jung speaks of an innate psychical structure indicating the need for mutual completion felt both by man and woman in a spiritual as well as a corporeal sense. Just as a human being is born with a virtual image of the world around him, as it were, so man has in his unconscious an image of woman known as "anima," and woman, in her attitude to man, is determined by an unconscious image, the "animus." Thus animus and anima designate contrasexual and complementary outward forms of psychic facts. It could also be expressed in this way: the anima compensates the male consciousness, and the animus the female. Jung came upon this state of affairs when engaged in investigating the processes of transformation of the unconscious soul and again as a result of the experiences within his own psyche. Thus the anima is actually the personification of the unconscious in man and is steeped in history and prehistory. In it are the contents of the past, and it replaces in man what he should know about his prehistory. Anima is all that past life which still remains alive in him.[62]

Related to the anima is the "persona," that is, the "mask" which a person puts on in order to play his social

The crowned hermaphrodite. From the illustrated *Tractatus qui dicitur Thomae Aquinatis de Alchimia*, about 1520. Leiden, University Library.

role, either that of a certain office or a certain class. Behind the persona is hidden the man who, for example, is known in public life through his office and his official manner. The relation between persona and anima is of a compensatory nature, that is to say, there is an adjustment between the mask-like, outward bearing of the persona and the anima in the unconscious. "The persona is a complicated system of relations between individual consciousness and society, fittingly enough a kind of mask,

59

designed on the one hand to make a definite impression upon others, and, on the other, to conceal the true nature of the individual . . . What then goes on behind the mask is called 'private life.' This painfully familiar division of consciousness into two figures, often preposterously different, is an incisive psychological operation that is bound to have repercussions on the unconscious."[63]

It is one of the tasks in the psychic process of maturing to see through this state of affairs and—insofar as this is possible—bring it into one's consciousness. Jung has repeatedly alluded to the great difficulty experienced in recognizing the nature of the anima and animus and also in overcoming the magic power with which the anima is linked. At the end of his chapter "Anima and Animus" in his book *The Relations between the Ego and the Unconscious* (1928), Jung actually thought it natural that not every reader would understand right away what is meant by animus and anima. Obviously he was contenting himself for the moment with creating the impression that what were involved were not metaphysical but empirical facts, although he intentionally avoided using an abstract and conceptual language to explain the matter: "It is far more to the point to give him some conception of what the actual possibilities of experience are. Nobody can really understand these things unless he has experienced them himself."[64]

Thus it is in experience that will be found the key to Jung's psychology. Mere intellectualization, playing with concepts, will not get at the fundamental facts. Anyone who looks into the elements of Jungian theory recognizes more and more that this body of concepts which at first seems strange, not to say abstruse, is based on a great wealth of experience. It is composed of the elements of Jung's personal experience, of that of his patients, and finally of that which has been deposited in the course of the history of mankind's ideas and which contributes to understanding by amplification: "The knowledge I was concerned with, or was seeking, still could not be found in the science of those days [that is, at the beginning of this century]. I myself had to undergo the original experience, and, moreover, try to plant the results of my experience in the soil of reality; otherwise they would have remained subjective assumptions without validity . . . All my works, all my creative activity, has come from those initial fantasies and dreams,"[65] Jung wrote as he looked back over his life. These lines provide fundamental criteria by means of which Jung's work can be assessed.

PSYCHOLOGICAL TYPES

For more than two thousand years the attempt has been made to capture man's image as it appears in body, mind, and soul by reducing it to a common denominator of typical characteristics. Early Greek thinkers and doctors have made such contributions as were possible in the light of their picture of the world and of man. Most widely known are the division into "four temperaments" according to their classification among the four elements of Empedocles, the theory of the humors in Hippocrates, or the kind of blood in Aristotle.

Alongside of these old conceptions of temperament, modern psychology has developed a wide range of theories of types. In the year 1921, thus almost contemporaneous with Rohrschach's *Theory of Types* and with Ernst Kretschmer's main work *Körperbau und Charakter*,

61

Carl Gustav Jung published his *Psychologischen Typen* (*Psychological Types*). Admittedly, this was not unexpected. For example, one can think of his lecture on psychological types which he delivered at the Psychology Congress in Munich in 1913. It will be found in the appendix to volume six in a reprint of the *Collected Works*, and provides insight into the growth of this theory.

His typology is based essentially on the results of his medical experiences. The criticisms made as one edition after another appeared led Jung in his preface to the seventh edition to remark that "my typology is the result of many years of practical experience, and such experience is, of course, not available to the academic psychologist . . . What I say in this book has been tested, so to speak, sentence by sentence, a hundred times in the practical

The Jung family. Château d'Oeux, 1917.

treatment of the sick, and it is on this treatment that my opinions were originally founded . . . The layman can hardly be criticized for thinking that certain statements sound rather strange or believing that my typology is the outcome of work done in a study in idyllic, undisturbed conditions . . ."[66] What characterizes Jung's theory is the point of view from which he looks at the type, that is, at an example or ideal which reproduces the character of a class or general group. As he does so, Jung seeks an answer to the question about the relation of the person concerned to the world around him, whether he turns towards or away from this world, whether he is inward- or outward-looking, whether he is an "introvert" or an "extravert."

At first sight, the method of looking at people under this double aspect seems almost simple, although it is undeniable that even these questions bring out quite fundamental attitudes. A detailed examination reveals that Jungian typology not only makes a wide differentiation of types possible but even takes account of the uniqueness of the individual trait which emerges from the type.

Jung observed two psychical "mechanisms" which are distinguished by the different goal they set themselves. Psychic energy directed outwards causes "extraversion," that is to say, a movement of interest towards the object. A movement of the interest away from the object towards the subject and his own psychological processes is characterized by Jung as "introversion." Thinking, feeling, and willing are at any time subordinated to one of these basic attitudes. Jung has himself seen a parallel in Goethe's idea of diastole (expansion) and systole (contraction). According to this, extraversion is marked by a diastolic outward-going to the object and its attainment, whereas introversion represents a systolic concentration and detachment of energy from the objects attained.

Jung defined both attitudes concisely in his *Über die*

The tower in Bollingen on the Lake of Zurich which Jung himself built for his own occupation and added to in subsequent years.

Psychologie des Unbewussten (1st ed., 1916; 5th ed., 1942) (ET *The Psychology of the Unconscious*, 1917, 1926, 1945). "The first attitude [i.e. that of the introvert] is normally characterized by a hesitant, reflective, retiring nature that keeps itself to itself, shrinks from objects, is always slightly on the defensive and prefers to hide behind mistrustful scrutiny. The second [i.e. that of the extravert] is normally characterized by an outgoing, candid, and accommodating nature that adapts itself easily to a given situation, quickly forms attachments, and, setting aside any possible misgivings, will often venture forth with careless confidence into unknown situations."[67] From this it follows that in the first case the subject, in the second, the object can claim the decisive significance. *Psychological Types*, an extensive work which has appeared in several editions, goes on to develop these two propositions, starting with an historical discussion of the problem of types as seen in classical antiquity, the Middle Ages, and in the various stages of modern times, and considering poetry in particular (Carl Spitteler, Goethe).

Jung, who was destined,[68] in no small part because of his own strongly pronounced basic attitude, to study this problem, emphasizes that the terms "extravert" and "introvert" should be understood without any value judgment. It is the personality itself which decides whether the positive or negative factors that can be deduced from either disposition predominate.

For the sake of accuracy, a clear distinction must be drawn between what Jung calls a "type" and what is meant by "attitude." The full meaning of the word "type" only applies when extraversion or introversion becomes a habitual characteristic and thus represents a constant. "Attitude," on the other hand, is the variable. It can change in the course of a lifetime, either because of a fundamental change in outlook or because of a "conversion." The accent can shift from the side of extraversion to that of introversion and vice versa. The typical is clearly the expression of the basic psychic structure at a given time.

Jung came across further distinguishing characteristics

when he saw that people with a strikingly similar basic psychic structure could appear markedly different. The possibilities of differentiation result from the part played by the "basic functions" noted by him. There are two rational functions, thinking and feeling; alongside these are two irrational functions, sensation and intuition. "I can give no *a priori* reason for selecting just these four as basic functions; I can only point out that this conception has shaped itself out of many years' experience. I differentiate these functions from one another because they are neither mutually relatable nor mutually reducible. The principle of thinking, for instance, is absolutely different from the principle of feeling, and so forth. I make a capital distinction between this concept of function and fantasy activity, or reverie, because, to my mind, fantasying is a peculiar form of activity which can manifest itself in all the four functions. In my view, both will and attention are entirely secondary psychic phenomena."[69] Considered from the standpoint of energy, a function is a manifestation of the libido, which in principle remains the same. Now, whereas these four functions are to be found in everybody, any particular person is distinguished by the predominance of one function, but also by the combined effect, the constellation of the other basic functions. Thus Jung speaks of types in which either thinking, feeling, intuition, or sensation is uppermost. "All the basic types can belong equally well to the one or the other class, according to the predominance of introversion or extraversion in the general attitude. A thinking type may belong either to the introverted or the extraverted class, and the same holds good for any other type. The differentiation into rational and irrational types is another point of view, and has nothing to do with introversion and extraversion."[70]

66

The *"Stein"* in Bollingen with figures and inscriptions, chiselled in by Jung himself.

Apart from the fact that practice must prove from case to case how Jung's typology can be employed, we only need to add what Jung means by rational and irrational: "The rational is the reasonable, that which accords with reason. I conceive reason as an attitude whose principle is to shape thought, feeling, and action in accordance with objective values. Objective values are established by the average experience of external facts on the one hand, and of inner psychological facts on the other . . . Thinking and feeling are rational functions insofar as they are decisively influenced by the motive of reflection. They attain their fullest significance when in fullest possible accord with the laws of reason. The irrational functions, on the contrary, are such as aim at pure perception, e.g., intuition and sensation: because, as far as possible, they are forced to dispense with the rational (which pre-supposes the exclusion of everything that is outside reason) in order to be able to reach the most complete perception of the whole course of events."[71]

Whereas sensation means basically what the senses tell us, what is the product of physical stimulus, intuiting, as Jung uses the word, is a kind of surmising perception, in which the unconscious plays a leading part. Jung was very reserved with regard to the irrational types as they are presented in his work *Psychological Types*. "The two types just depicted are almost inaccessible to external judgment. Because they are introverted and have in consequence a somewhat meager capacity or willingness for expression, they offer but a frail handle for a telling criticism."[72]

What results can the efforts of the psychologist show when essential features of the psyche of such people are concealed behind a screen of apathy, uncertainty, and failure to communicate? Obviously it depends on the standpoint of the critic. "From an extraverted and rationalistic standpoint, such types are indeed the most fruitless of men. But, viewed from a higher standpoint, such men are living evidence of the fact that this rich and varied world with its overflowing and intoxicating life is not purely external, but also exists within. These types are admittedly one-sided demonstrations of Nature, but they are an educational experience for the man who refuses to be blinded by the intellectual mode of the day. In their own way, men with such an attitude are educators and promoters of culture . . ."[73]

No doubt such an argument can only be put forward by

someone who has had experiences stemming from a related basic psychic structure. And, conversely, an estimate of Jungian psychology could be determined by typological factors.

Heinz Remplein, who in his *Psychologie der Persönlichkeit* discusses in detail the attitude- and function-types found in Jung's work, does indeed make limitations in calling attention to the Jungian characteristics which are to be found throughout his psychological work. He remarks rightly that Jung's typology can only be fully understood and appreciated in the light of all he wrote. However, Remplein recognizes also that, in spite of these doubts, there could be only admiration for the dynamic force which Jungian typology possessed more than any other, because it related to consciousness the unconscious and its constant tension. And he added that there was no doubt that Jung's typology had long since proved its value in the hands of those who had fully mastered it, both in psychotherapy and in diagnosis.

However, Jung has certainly not expressed satisfaction with his elucidation of the problem of types. Jung always endeavored to respect human individuality insofar as it was unique, untransferable, and incomparable. In any case, it never occurred to him to use psychological type-labels as a means of standardizing or cataloguing the human personality. Typology was for him only a means to an end, a valuable construct, but one which he would never allow to come between himself and anyone else. And so Jung himself felt uneasy about what had resulted in 1912/13 from his reflections on his relations with Freud and Adler, which had first manifested itself on the occasion of the lecture delivered at the Munich Congress which has already been mentioned, and had then been represented in his mature work *Psychological Types*. When reviewing the results of many years of research, Jung came to see that "every judgment made by an individual is conditioned by his personality type and that every point of view is necessarily relative. This raised the question of the unity which must compensate this diversity."[74]

Quite new perspectives opened up for Jung when he became interested in Asiatic thought and particularly that pertaining to ancient China. His meeting with that great Sinologist, Richard Wilhelm, and his study of his works *Geheimnis der Goldenen Blüte* (ET *Secret of the Golden Flower*) and *I Ching*, gave Jung's work a new impulse. To it belongs the idea of "acausal parallelism"; Jung also uses the word "synchronicity" to mean an explanatory principle other than that of causality which would permit of an interpretation from their sense content of psychic and physical events running parallel to one another. In addition, his preoccupation with Oriental thought awoke in Jung the need to know more about the nature of alchemy, a long-since forgotten and misunderstood kind of research which he hoped to use in his investigations of the psyche. We shall return to this later.

Since Jung's researches into the problem of attitude type had been set in motion by the differing theoretical standpoints of Freud and Adler, it is not without interest to see what Jung thought about their respective positions. At the same time, this will throw light on the way he tried to understand other people's convictions which he himself was unable to share. In his book *The Psychology of the Unconscious*, which ran into a fifth edition in 1941, and is based on an essay published in 1912 under the title "*Neue Bahnen in der Psychologie*" ("New Paths in Psychology"), Jung reflects on the incompatibility of the theories of Freud and Adler and acknowledges that "the Freudian theory is attractively simple, so much so that it almost

70

Richard Wilhelm.

pains one if anybody drives in the wedge of a contrary
assertion. But the same is true of Adler's theory. It too is
of illuminating simplicity and explains just as much as the
Freudian theory. No wonder, then, that the adherents of
both schools obstinately cling to their one-sided truths.''[75]
Jung understands the arguments of both men very well,
indeed, he is in a position to judge that both theories are
in large measure correct. Thus the difficulty lies in the fact
that an alternative solution is *a priori* excluded. Jung's
answer is precisely that typology which he had developed

step by step and by means of which the antithesis in the psychic attitudes of Adler and Freud can be explained: "This difference can hardly be anything else but a difference of temperament, a contrast between two types of mentality, one of which finds the determining agency pre-eminently in the subject, the other in the object . . ."[76]

What Jung found again and again in his medical practice provided him with a classical example from among the wealth of the many types of attitudes in this Freud-Adler controversy. This example—Jung himself points to a series of others—also shows that his typology eminently serves as an aid to understanding figures in intellectual life. The law according to which a contemporary or historical figure is approached can thus be seen in one important respect, although the mystery of individuality and fate still remains hidden. What Jung was already writing about psychological types in the *Zeitschrift für Menschenkunde* in the year 1925 is still valid today: "Classification does not explain the individual soul. Nevertheless, an understanding of psychological types opens the way to a better understanding of human psychology in general."[77]

Jung adhered to this statement, which bears witness to his modesty. Again and again he said that, when dealing as a psychotherapist with a patient, he never had the feeling that he was an authority entitled to claim that he knew anything about the other's individuality or even to violate a fellow being's area of independence. Ten years later the sexagenarian wrote: "I am in no position to judge the whole of the personality before me. I cannot say anything valid about him except insofar as he approximates to the 'universal man.' But since all life is to be found only in individual form, and I myself can assert of another individuality only what I find in my own, I am in constant danger either of doing violence to the other person or of succumbing to his influence. If I wish to treat another individual psychologically at all, I must for better of worse give up all pretensions to superior knowledge, all authority and desire to influence. I must perforce adopt a dialectical procedure consisting in a comparison of our mutual findings."[78]

PSYCHOLOGY AND RELIGION

Modern psychological research has shown that it needed to pay special attention to religious questions. Even Sigmund Freud, who called himself an absolutely godless Jew and, even in his old age, insisted on an attitude of complete rejection of religion in every form and however diluted, recognized that religion could not be disposed of as an "illusion." His basic thinking and the circumstances of his life, therefore, allowed him at least to make pronouncements about religion which were full of skepticism. His surmises did not deceive him.

As for Jung, the relation between psychology and religion (which must not be regarded as synonymous with theology) is positive from the start, although he too in this respect went through phases of transformation. While he could evidently never find any sympathy for the preaching about Jesus of the established Church (for example: "All that about Lord Jesus was always suspect to me and I never really believed it"[79]), yet Jung did have direct religious experiences. In his autobiographical notes he says of the time when he was going to the Gymnasium: "Suddenly I understood that God was, for me at least, one of the most

The risen Christ as a symbol of the *filius philosophorum*. From the *Rosarium Philosophorum* (Frankfurt, 1550).

certain and immediate experiences.''[80] And alongside is the note that the farther he got away from the Church, the better he felt.

If one interprets these disclosures correctly—and, after all, they are to be found in an illuminating context—this receptivity of Jung for religious matters can scarcely, if at all, be traced back to his father's vocation as parson. Rather, one gets the impression that the religious outlook of the growing boy actually developed in opposition to the theological type which his father represented and which was alien to religion. If Jung became neither a traditional mystic nor a religious leader, he had in his nature a predisposition towards the *homo religiosus.* He knew with Goethe's Faust (he came to value *Faust* at an early age, together with the Gospel according to Saint John) that in the last resort it is not the "parchment" which is the "holy well" giving refreshment to the seeker, but that the divine word is to be heard in the fount of one's own soul.

Anyone who wants to learn about Jung's relation to religion as seen in his works should look not only at those books whose titles suggest that they deal expressly with this subject. The results would be relatively meager. Reference to the Terry Lectures, *Psychology and Religion,* or to the late work *Antwort auf Hiob* (ET *Answer to Job,* 1952), would be far from sufficient to gain an adequate picture. Nevertheless, there are in these works important pronouncements, for example, about what he understands by religion and why, as a psychologist, he deals with it so intensively: "Religion, as the Latin word denotes, is a careful and scrupulous observation of what Rudolf Otto (in *The Idea of the Holy*) aptly termed the '*numinosum,*' that is, a dynamic agency or effect not caused by an arbitrary act of the will. On the contrary, it seizes and controls the human subject, who is always rather its victim than its creator. The '*numinosum*'—whatever its cause may be—is an experience of the subject independent of his will."[81] Jung recognizes that religion is "incontestably one of the earliest and most universal expressions of the human mind," and therefore it is obvious "that any psychology which touches upon the psychological structure of human personality cannot avoid taking note of the fact that religion is not only a sociological and historical phenome-
75

non, but also something of considerable personal concern to a great number of individuals."[82]

Anyone who takes up the *Answer to Job* without any preparation—and this can hardly be recommended—will inevitably find himself saying that the author of a book which betrays such an intimate knowledge of theological and religious matters cannot have come upon the subject casually. This fact will certainly be an obstacle for not a few of his readers. The evangelical theologian Hans Schär is right in remarking in his informative monograph *Religion and Soul in the Psychology of C. G. Jung* that "the theologian who gets absorbed in Jung will be astonished again and again at the formidable and comprehensive knowledge Jung possesses, both of Christianity and of the religions outside it. In this respect his knowledge is unique. Very few theologians or laymen have so wide a knowledge of religious life in all its forms as Jung has . . . Even those who cannot agree with all of Jung's interpretations must needs acknowledge his right to treat of religion."[83] And yet, as we have said, Jung does not make this knowledge and discussion of religion an end in itself; what he has directly experienced always serves to justify what he does. Josef Rudin, the Zürich Catholic theologian and psychotherapist, spoke therefore of postulates which essentially determined Jung's basic attitudes to the world, life, and God, when he said that three postulates—the primacy of experience, the reality of the soul, and his knowledge of wholeness—made it clear that Jung's separation from Freud did not inevitably proceed from an unresolved Oedipus complex, but that most profound forces developing from his own personal structure had led him to his own personal view of man, the world, and God.[84]

Because of his fundamental attitude, the judgment

Job being beaten by Satan. Woodcut from the *Feldtbuch der Wundtarzney*
by H. v. Gersdoff, 1590.

would be appropriate for Jung which William James pronounced on his own position as scientist when he said that he was devout ("Our scientific temper is devout," *Pragmatism*, 1911, pp. 14 ff.). This religious component was always present, whether Jung was following the transformation process of the psyche in alchemistic folio volumes or commenting on the doctrine of the East; whether he was interpreting politico-social relations (for example, events during the Third Reich), or reporting what his mood was when, as a young man, he communed with nature. Religion appeared to him "to be a peculiar attitude of mind which could be formulated in accordance with the original use of the word *'religio,'* which means a careful consideration and observation of certain dynamic factors that are conceived as 'powers': spirits, daemons, gods, laws, ideals, or whatever name man has given to such factors in his world as he has found powerful, dangerous, or helpful enough to be taken into careful consideration, or grand, beautiful, and meaningful enough to be devoutly worshipped and loved."[85] Religion considered in this way is by no means only the object or need of "religious natures." It can certainly not be measured by asking whether and to what extent any person performs "religious duties" in a community possessing a faith or a creed. In this respect Jung approximates to the conception of Tertullian, a Father of the Church, who said: *"Anima naturaliter christiana"* ("the soul is by nature Christian"), insofar as he believes that a natural religious function is inherent in the human soul.

Intelligibly enough, the depth psychologist had repeatedly to refute the reproach that his thesis about the reality of the soul was supporting a kind of "psychologism," that his conception, according to which there were psychic factors corresponding to divine or religious figures, must be considered debasement, and that religious experiences were "not only psychological" and therefore not to be considered exclusively with the means of psychology. And so theologians occasionally point out that the psychic is "only" nature, meaning by that: earthbound, sinful, and therefore God-forsaken if not contrary to God.

Capture of the Leviathan with the fishing rod in seven parts of the tribe of Jesse and the crucifix as bait. From the *Hortus deliciarum* of Herrad von Landsberg, about 1180.

To these critics Jung replied that they had deliberately ignored his reference to the psychic origin of religious phenomena which had been furnished in *Psychology and Religion*. And in return he asked: "How do we know so much about the psyche that we can say 'only' psychic? For this is how Western man, whose soul is evidently of 'little worth,' speaks and thinks. If much were in his soul, he would speak of it with reverence. But since he does not do so, we can only conclude that there is nothing of value in it. Not that this is necessarily so always and everywhere, but only with people who put nothing into their souls and have 'all God outside.' (A little more Meister Eckhart would be a very good thing sometimes!)"[86]

Jung also warns against a debasement of the soul by an exclusively religious projection into cult and dogma and adds that, when this happens, the religious life petrifies in external matters and formalities. The most recent history of theology with its partly traditional and denominational, partly modern and intellectualistic positions—and both are to be found in particularly Protestantism—shows how correct the statements of the psychologist are. "But if the soul no longer has any part to play, religious life congeals into externals and formalities. However we may picture the relationship between God and soul, one thing is certain, that the soul cannot be 'nothing but.' On the contrary, it has the dignity of an entity endowed with consciousness of a relationship to Deity. Even if it were only the relationship of a drop of water to the sea."[87]

Of course, one should guard against overrating what Jung says, especially where he is laying great emphasis on thinking by analogy. But undoubtedly one must take seriously the argument that "it would be blasphemy to assert that God can manifest himself everywhere save only in the human soul."[88]

Here Jung revises some pronouncements which he had made too hastily: "It would be going perhaps too far to speak of an affinity; but at all events the soul must contain in itself the faculty of relationship to God, i.e., a correspondence, otherwise a connection could never come about."[89] Thinking of his fellow countryman Karl Barth he adds the footnote: "It is therefore quite unthinkable psychologically for God to be simply the 'wholly other,' for a 'wholly other' could never be one of the soul's deepest and closest intimates—which is precisely what God is. The only statements concerning the God image that have psychological validity are either paradoxes or antinomies."[90]

In what does the psychologist see some possiblity of a relationship between God and the soul, and in what a correspondence? Jung's answer is unequivocal: it is the archetype of the God image in the soul. "The archetype of religious notions has, like every instinct, its specific energy which it does not lose even if consciousness ignores it. As one can suppose with the greatest probability that every human being possesses all the average human functions and qualities, one can also expect the presence of the normal religious factors or archetypes, and this expectation does not deceive, as can easily be seen." But how is it when a conscious and deliberate problem of faith arises? Jung s reply is that anyone who succeeds in discarding one covering of faith can only do so because there is another at hand . . . Nobody can escape the prejudice of being human."[91]

In this connection, Jung speaks once again of the expression "psychic wholeness." It is the self appearing in the so-called quaternity. The application of the comparative method has shown "that the quaternity is a more or less direct representation of the God who is manifest in his

81

The *Anthropos* and the four elements. From a Russian manuscript of the eighteenth century. From a private collection.

creation. We might, therefore, conclude that the symbol spontaneously produced in the dreams of modern people means something similar."[92] Jung points to a reflection of the "essential identity of God and man" and calls it "the God within." If any misunderstanding is to be avoided, this name must be taken strictly as a pronouncement which is psychological and not in any way theological or religious-mystical. For "it would be a regrettable mistake if anybody should take my observations as a kind of proof of the existence of God. They only prove the existence of an archetypal God image, which to my mind is the most we can assert about God psychologically. But as it is a very important and influential archetype, its relatively frequent occurrence seems to be a noteworthy fact for any *theologia naturalis*. And since experience of this archetype has the quality of numinosity, often in very high degree, it comes into the category of religious experience.''[93]

As a scientist making use of experience, Jung had to admit that the analogy in question did not reappear in all, nor even in the majority of cases known to him. Nevertheless, he can point to a series of 400 dreams in which the quaternity factor appeared 71 times. In *Psychology and Alchemy* these dreams are discussed in detail and he adds that he, like his colleagues, had seen so many cases in which the same kind of symbolism was developed that they could no longer doubt its existence.

The reproach that Jung has published his observations prematurely is totally without foundation. His investigations of this kind go back to the time after his break with Freud, that is, to around 1914. Jung allowed fourteen years to elapse, which were spent in collecting the material and checking his results, before, in the commentary on *The Secret of the Golden Flower* (1929), he published anything about them. As one can see, the question of the "God within," the archetype God, is closely connected with his work on alchemistic experiences in the West and the East. So closely linked together are the works of Jung. The results support one another.

In view of the importance of the matter brought to light by depth psychology, why does modern man not directly perceive these facts? Why does the reflection of the archetypal God image appear only in his dreams, that is, in the products of the unconscious?

Jung, who studied the contrast between Western and Asiatic spirituality intensively, points chiefly to the difference of attitude in the West and the East with regard to the

The phoenix as a symbol of the resurrection. From Boschius, *Ars Symbolica* (Augsburg, 1702).

soul. "Western man is held in thrall by the 'ten thousand things'; he sees only particulars, he is ego-bound and thing-bound, and unaware of the deep root of all being. Eastern man, on the other hand, experiences the world of particulars, and even his own ego, like a dream; he is rooted essentially in the 'Ground,' which attracts him so powerfully that his relations with the world are relativized to a degree that is often incomprehensible to us. The Western attitude, with its emphasis on the object, tends to fix the ideal—Christ—in its outward aspect and thus to rob it of its mysterious relationship to the inner man. It is this prejudice, for instance, which impels the Protestant interpreters of the Bible to interpret '*entos hymin*' (referring to the kingdom of God) as 'among you' instead of 'within you.'"[94] The mediator seen in picture or symbol or believed in, remains "outside"; at best he is imitated, but there is no transformation of the inmost being. "It may easily happen, therefore, that a Christian who believes in all the sacred figures is still undeveloped and unchanged in his inmost soul because he has 'all God outside' and does not experience him in the soul. His deciding motives, his ruling interests and impulses, do not spring from the sphere of Christianity but from the unconscious and undeveloped psyche, which is as pagan and archaic as ever."[95]

Jung has every reason to administer a severe rebuke to Christianity, especially in its Protestant form. It is ultimately a lack of genuine religiosity that the psychologist diagnoses. "Christian civilization has proved hollow to a terrifying degree: it is all veneer, but the inner man has remained untouched and therefore unchanged. His soul is out of key with his external beliefs."[96] Jung recommends that the Christian mission take a new direction, that it start afresh. It must be understood that the "mysterious magnum" is not only of value in itself; it must be realized that this mystery is founded in the human soul. Psychology, he says, can help to solve this problem. Here too Jung guards against any unauthorized trespass by covering himself against the misunderstanding that psychology was endeavoring to insinuate a new and possibly heretical doctrine. Since the relation of the soul to what is outwardly believed and preached is only revealed by inward experience, the task of psychology is to teach how to see realities and, as far as is possible, how to understand them. The very nature of science preserved psychology from a partisan appraisal of religious symbols. Hence Jung sees Christ as an extremely important symbol of the self; but he knows, too, that in the religions of the East, for example, the archetype of the self is symbolized by other names of God or founders.

85

How are the perspectives of psychology and religion related? Jung's answer is as follows: "The religious point of view, understandably enough, puts the accent on the imprinter, whereas scientific psychology emphasizes the *typos,* the imprint—the only thing it can understand. The religious point of view understands the imprint as the working of an imprinter; the scientific point of view understands it as the symbol of an unknown and incomprehensible content. Since the *typos* is less definite and more variegated than any of the figures postulated by religion, psychology is compelled by its empirical material to express the *typos* by means of a terminology not bound by time, place, or milieu."[97] The word "self," which simultaneously expresses the essence of the union of opposites, satisfies this demand.

Jung has been asked why he spoke at all of the God image and why he used religious categories to represent psychic relationships. (As is well known, the concept plays an important part, especially with the Fathers of the Church in the early centuries. Their teaching was in accordance with Jewish tradition, which for its part was based on the first biblical report of the creation—Genesis 1, 26 f.—where it is said that, imprinted in the soul is *"imago dei,"* that is, the image of God.) Jung's answer, which takes various forms in different places in his collected works, runs as follows: "The God image is not something invented, it is an experience that comes upon man spontaneously—as anyone can see for himself unless he is blinded to the truth by theories and prejudice."[98]

In his work *Relations between the Ego and the Unconscious,* an account is given of a female patient (one example of several) whom the psychiatrist describes as critical and agnostic, and he adds that "her idea of a possible deity had long since passed into the realm of the inconceivable, that

86

is, had dwindled into a complete abstraction." In marked contrast is what her dream life shows: "Out of the purely personal form the dreams develop an archaic God image that is infinitely far from the conscious idea of God." In *Psychology and Alchemy* Jung remarks that every archetype is capable of infinite development and differentiation, and this includes the possibility that the archetype of the God image can remain on an undeveloped, archaic level while the intellect can be highly developed.

The objection has also been raised that Jung's interpretation, which is related to the subject of the dreamer (he calls it interpretation on the subject level), represents a philosophical problem and ceases therefore to be scientific. The reply to this attack is that "it does not surprise

Christ as *Anthropos,* standing on the globe and surrounded by the four elements. From *Le proprietaire des choses* by Barthélemy de Glanville, 1487.

me that psychology debouches into philosophy, for the thinking that underlies philosophy is after all a psychic activity which, as such, is the proper study of psychology. I always think of psychology as encompassing the whole of the psyche, and that includes philosophy and theology and many other things besides. For underlying all philosophies and all religions are the facts of the human soul, which may ultimately be the arbiters of truth and error.''[99]

From the starting point of the God-image of the divine man, Jung once went into the cause which—with others—may have been decisive for the surprisingly rapid expansion of Christianity in the first three centuries. His conclusion was that "Christ would never have made the impression he did on his followers if he had not expressed something that was alive and at work in their unconscious. Christianity would never have spread through the pagan world with such astonishing rapidity had its ideas not found an analogous psychic readiness to receive them.''[100]

Before Jung—in the *Answer to Job*—endeavored to explain this affinity between certain contents of the unconscious and the figure of the saviour, he mentioned it in another place as well. In *Symbols of the Mind* he added that "Christ could only have an effect because of the *consensus generalis* of unconscious expectation," and that the "archetype of the self in every soul had responded to this message so that the concrete rabbi Jesus was assimilated in the shortest time by the constellated archetype.''[101] According to Jung, this readiness was provided in the link between the unconscious and the saviour precisely in the archetype of the divine man. Here we shall only note that in the work *Aion* important symbolic-historical materials are to be found dealing with this question. The reiterated indication that all this was dealing primarily with the self and man's growing to wholeness, and only secondarily with attempts at an interpretation of theological matters seems unnecessary.

To sum up Jung's contribution to the relation of psychology and religion, in the words of Hans Schär: "All those who are concerned with religion today must take account of Jung's work. There is no point in retracing our steps behind him; we can only go forward along the trail he has blazed."[102]

ALCHEMY AND THE STUDY OF THE PSYCHE

Anyone who comes unprepared to Jung's work is struck by the frequent and detailed quotations of alchemistic symbols and textual examples. They serve to remind one of that old spiritual attitude, now almost forgotten, which underlay not only the study of prescientific chemistry but primarily a spiritual path of cognition involving issues such as transmutation and the transformation or improvement of one's own being, that is to say, knowledge of oneself as well as of the world. Anyone following this path—before alchemy degenerated into the attempt to make gold and fell into disrepute—wanted to prepare the *lapis philosophorum*, the "philosophers' stone" and the "elixir of life." The doctor and poet Alexander von Bernus, one of the very few who in the present time still took this path, said that the background of alchemy was initiation, a training in mysteries going back thousands of years, and that, rooted in pre-Christian ages in the psychic outlook of the Egyptians, the Chaldees, and the Hellenes, and later brought from the Orient to the West by Arab culture, it was tinged

with the substance of Christianity. Von Bernus added that certainly the idea of transmutation was at the center of this alchemistic way, and not the transformation of metals but the inward mystical process of transmutation of which the external chemical and physical transformation of metal was only the visible and outward form of what has happened inside material things. Alexander von Bernus is the author of *Alchimie und Heilkunst* (Nuremberg, 1948).

Jung's interest was directed towards neither this early phase in the history of chemistry and metallurgy nor the spiritual exercise which the alchemist had in mind when he used chemical images and processes. Jung was concerned here too with fulfilling the psychiatrist's mission. His task lay in utilizing for psychotherapy that extremely abundant but generally almost inaccessible supply of images, symbols, recipes, and descriptions furnished by the alchemists of late antiquity and the Middle Ages, of the East and of the West. How did he come to do this? He wrote: "As my life entered its second half, I was already embarked on the confrontation with the contents of the unconscious. My work on this was an extremely long-drawn-out affair, and it was only after some twenty years of it that I reached some degree in understanding of my fantasies." Jung felt the need to clarify what was seen and experienced in dreams on the lines of his premises; for he wrote that "analytical psychology is fundamentally a natural science, but it is subject far more than any other science to the personal bias of the observer. The psychologist must depend therefore in the highest degree upon historical and literary parallels if he wishes to exclude at least the crudest errors in judgment."[103]

It was after the First World War, until about 1926, that Jung, with this purpose in mind, seriously studied the fragmentary traditions of pre-Christian Gnosis. He thought that its votaries had come upon the "primal world of the unconscious." And therefore he considered that Gnosticism could yield appropriate information. The fragmentary character of Gnostic tradition which, moreover,

Alchemists at work. Various stages of the process. Sol appears at the bottom, bringing the Golden Flower. From the *Mutus Liber*, 1677.

in his time was still only to be found in the hostile writings of the Church Fathers—more extensive and authentic Gnostic documents were discovered and published only in the 1930's-40's[104]—led Jung to realize that the Gnostics were too remote in time for his purpose and that he could not therefore make use of their experiences. He wrote that "the tradition that might have connected Gnosis with the present seemed to have been severed, and for a long time it proved impossible to find any bridge that led from Gnosticism—or neo-Platonism—to the contemporary world."[105]

In 1926 a dream led him on to the right track. He felt himself taken back into the seventeenth century, to the time when alchemy had already passed its climax in the West. But Jung remembered a book on the subject by the psychoanalyst Herbert Silberer (*Probleme der Mystik und ihrer Symbolik*, Vienna, 1914), in which an attempt had been made to interpret alchemistic literature, especially that of the seventeenth century, on the foundations of Sigmund Freud's theory. When Jung began to understand the significance of alchemy for the elucidation of his own special problems, he recognized that "it represented the historical link with Gnosticism, and that a continuity therefore existed between past and present. Grounded in the natural philosophy of the Middle Ages, alchemy formed the bridge on the one hand into the past, to Gnosticism, and on the other into the future, to the modern psychology of the unconscious."[106] It must be borne in mind here that Jung was not, however, interested in a rehabilitation of alchemy as such. This is further underlined by the opinion of Alexander von Bernus who commends Jung's work as a pioneering feat "for any future psychic research," but, at the same time, denies that Jung has any competence to judge the work of the alchemists. This criticism by the modern alchemist will of course affect the depth psychologist all the less because he really wanted to get to the bottom of those facts by virtue of which patients' dreams and hallucinations strikingly reminded him of hermetic-alchemistic symbolism or even reproduced it. In his lengthy work *Psychology and Alchemy* (1944), which even wins the alchemy expert's approval by its careful and abundant selection of 270 illustrations, such dreams are given, commented upon, and confronted with

From one of Jung's alchemical notebooks.

relevant alchemistic ideas after the manner of Jungian amplification.

But much research had to be done before *Psychology and Alchemy* could be written and made available to the public. This necessitated a thorough familiarization with material, both in prose and pictures, which was chiefly difficult of access, laborious to gather, and not at all easy to interpret. These strange writings, which Jung used for numerous works, are to be found in the original editions of Jung's studies. What was decisive for Jung's understanding of alchemy was his meeting with the Sinologist Richard Wilhelm. In 1928 he received Wilhelm's translation of the *Golden Flower*, a treatise from the realm of old Chinese alchemy, and then said that "light on the nature of alchemy began to come to me only after I had read the text of the *Golden Flower*. I was stirred by the desire to become more closely acquainted with the alchemical texts."[107] Jung wrote a European commentary and published the book jointly with Wilhelm in 1929. In the conclusion will be found the following words: "The purpose of my commentary is to attempt to build a bridge of psychological understanding between East and West."[108] (We shall later have more to say about the necessity, as Jung saw it, to build a bridge between the thought of East and West.) That confrontation of psychology with religious problems, which plays an extremely important part in Jung's work, and his study of Paracelsus, to which the essays *Paracelsica* (1942) refer, finally led Jung to publish something about alchemy in its relation to religion and psychology. The following reference is important: "With that I had at last reached the ground which underlay my own experiences of the years 1913 to 1917; for the process through which I had passed at that time corresponded to the process of alchemical transformation discussed in *Psychology and Alchemy*."[109]

One is struck by the fact that Jung could decide only after some hesitation to publish—at least by way of suggestion—the results of observations in his practice and of himself. "One cannot be too cautious in these matters for what with the imitative urge and a positively morbid avidity to possess themselves of outlandish feathers and deck themselves out in this exotic plumage, far too many people are misled into snatching at such 'magical' ideas and applying them externally, like an ointment."[110] It is for the same reason that for many years he concealed even from his closest collaborators his special investigations and studies. Not until 1935, on the occasion of an Eranos conference held in Ascona and promoted by Olga Fröbe-Kapteyn did he deliver a lecture on "Traumsymbole des Individuationsprozesses," thereby affording insight into the problem. "Die Erlösungsvorstellungen in der Alchemie" followed one year later in similar circumstances. Jung was able to demonstrate how a series of dream experiences could be shown to have a parallel with various stations on the alchemistic way. These and similar works finally led by way of *Psychology and Alchemy* to the *Mysterium Coniunctionis* (1955-57) in three volumes, which can be regarded as

Laboratory: alchemists at work. From the *Mutus Liber*, 1677.

96

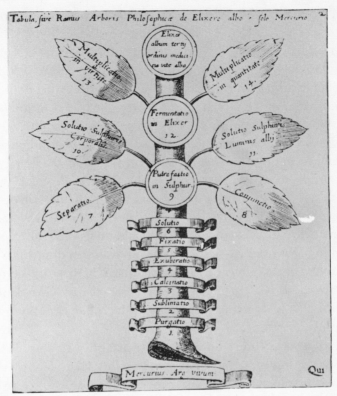

The twelve alchemical operations represented as an *arbor philosophica.*

the keystone of Jung's research on the subject of the separation and conjunction of psychical opposites in alchemy.

The significance of alchemy for Jung's psychology is found in the underlying psychic reality. The alchemist in front of his work (*opus alchimicum*) sees himself as someone who cannot and will not remain as he is at present. He wishes to undergo a transformation. That is why Gerhard Dorn (Dorneus), a disciple of Paracelsus in the sixteenth century, demands point-blank: *"Transmutemini in vivos philosophicos!"* ("Change yourselves into living philosoph-

97

ical stones!''), that is, find yourselves the wise man's stone or make ready for it by changing your own being! The procedures to be followed with the *"prima materia,"* that is, with the original, unchanged substance, and which can be represented in various stages and with quite definite manifestations (e.g. changing colors), thus refer ultimately to the alchemist himself. He himself must go through a process of initiation which can be expressed in images of ancient chemistry. The process represented therein corresponds to a way of salvation the effects of which pass from the process of transformation within the person on to matter; after the mystical fact comes the chemical fact, transforming substances. The alchemists of the West coming from the Rosicrucian Order attempted in this way to make intelligible to the world the Christ story of the incarnation (Christ made flesh). For them Christianity is not just a doctrine; it is a fact which has generated an impulse.

However, Jung—and he is constantly criticized for it—is not interested in what may possibly take place on the plane of transpsychic reality, for instance, in the realm of chemistry. Here too, for him, the only fact and reality to be investigated is the psychic, because every spiritual fact, and therefore the alchemistic theory as well, signifies a psychic reality and is brought into consciousness by the agency of the psyche. Jung's discovery lies in the observation that the unconscious also goes through processes which are to an astonishing degree like those of the alchemists in their image content. In the accounts of the alchemists, Jung sees an expression or, more precisely, a projection of the archetypal or the collective unconscious. The unconscious is projected on to matter.

What Jung understands here by projection is expressed in *Psychology and Alchemy* as follows: "Everything unknown and empty is filled with psychological projection; it

Hermaphroditus with the winged ball of chaos, the seven planets, and the dragon. From *Viatorum Spagyricum* by H. Jamsthaler (Frankfurt, 1625).

is as if the investigator's own psychic background were mirrored in the darkness. What he sees in matter, or thinks he can see, is chiefly the data of his own consciousness which he is projecting into it. In other words, he encounters in matter, as apparently belonging to it, certain qualities and potential meanings of whose psychic nature he is entirely unconscious. This is particularly true of classical alchemy, when empirical science and mystical philosophy were more or less undifferentiated.''[111]

Psychology and Alchemy provides most impressive documentation of the way in which Jung studied chiefly the religious-psychological problem of alchemy. This art which had fallen into oblivion since the Age of Enlightenment and had been pushed aside by modern science had first of all to be ''dug out'' again by him and reconstructed in its elements before it could serve the psychiatrist's purpose. This achievement alone, adding as it does to our knowledge of the history of culture and thought, deserves recognition and approval. The relevant texts and the engravings illustrating them were put together under the strict observance of an esoteric discipline. Secrecy had to be guarded. Therefore a maze of pictures and symbols had to be worked through before a clear idea of what was actually meant could be obtained.

Jung introduces the reader into the alchemistic notions of salvation. He points out the goal of alchemistic activity as well as its individual phases. Then the psychic nature of this activity is demonstrated. Jung is of the opinion that ''while working on his chemical experiments the [alchemist] operator had certain psychic experiences which appeared to him as the particular behavior of the chemical process. Since it was a question of projection, he was naturally unconscious of the fact that the experience had nothing to do with matter itself (that is, with matter as we know it today). He experienced his projection as a property of matter, but what he was in reality experiencing was his own unconscious.''[112] It is another question whether the material-supramaterial observations of the alchemists can be suitably and comprehensively interpreted by means of the Jungian category of the unconscious. In fact, Jung can point to some descriptions of his authorities according to which they report about corresponding experiences (e.g. visions) partly in realistic, partly in metaphysical form. Besides this, Jung's reference to the numerous figures and motives of the alchemical

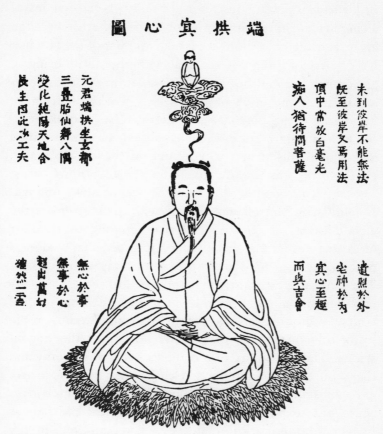

圖心宺拱端

未到彼岸不能無法
既至彼岸又焉用法
頂中常放白毫光
痴人猶待問菩薩

長生因此次工夫
没化純陽天地含
三叠胎仙舞八個
元君端拱坐玄都

道烈於外
宅神於為
宺心至趣
而與吉會

湟然二含
起此萬幻
無事於心
無心於事

Meditation: third stage. From *The Secret of the Golden Flower*.

process which have a religious imprint and which are placed in a central position deserves attention. Thus, for example, the "philosophical stone" (*lapis philosophorum*) which has to be prepared is placed in parallel to Christ. And, since the Christ image, as well as the goal of that activity, corresponds to individuation and is concerned with psychic wholeness, Jung's interpretation of the divine-man archetype finds important support in alchemy.

But is it worthwhile to pay more attention to alchemy, alien as it is to the consciousness of the present day, in

101

order to learn about Jung's psychology? Is the reading of alchemical writing with all its obscurities necessary? The answer to such questions must take account of the fact that large parts of Jung's work deal with the deciphering of alchemistic symbolism, and elements from these contents are to be found in all of Jung's later works. Even more important is the personal and fateful relation of Jung to the alchemical tradition which has already been mentioned and which caused him to continue his devoted research even during his voyage to India (1938). In *Memories, Dreams, Reflections* there is a description of how Jung had to familiarize himself step by step with the meaning of the alchemical style. "It was a task that kept me absorbed for more than a decade. I had very soon seen that analytical psychology coincided in a most curious way with alchemy. The experiences of the alchemists were, in a sense, my experience, and their world was my world. This was, of course, a momentous discovery: I had stumbled upon the historical counterpart of my psychology of the unconscious. The possibility of a comparison with alchemy and the uninterrupted intellectual chain back to Gnosticism gave substance to my psychology. When I poured over these old texts, everything fell into place: the fantasy images, the empirical material I had gathered in my practice, and the conclusions I had drawn from it . . ."[113]

JUNG AND EASTERN THOUGHT

It is pointed out with a certain justification that Jung has made a vital contribution to increasing the interest of the Westerner in the spirituality of Asia. Undoubtedly this is not just connected with the fact that Jung was helped when deciphering alchemical dream symbols by the Sino-logical work of Richard Wilhelm. Jung had to study the intellectual and religious traditions of the East because of his need for a complete view of the world and man. The Oriental had a different structure of consciousness going back into the psychic past, and the forms this took seemed to him to be suitable for throwing light on certain psychic products of the Westerner. Rudyard Kipling's well-known and much quoted thesis from the year 1889: "Oh, East is East, and West is West, and never the twain shall meet," was not one to which Jung would ever have been willing to subscribe. In fact, his work is a proof of the possibility of a meeting of East and West.

In this endeavor Jung was not spared the reproach of confusing a world outlook with religion. "The strongest force . . . which contributes to the creation of a syncretic basic mood is the school founded by Carl Gustav Jung . . . In any case Jung's psychology contributes directly or indirectly to the creation of a religious eclecticism in which the most varied religious conceptions are assembled without any possibility of a really intellectual judgment"; that is what the ecumenical theologian Willem A. Visser 't Hooft wrote in *Kein anderer Name* (Basle, 1965). Ernst Benn, the historian of ideas, supports this criticism from another starting point. Moreover, the fear is expressed that, in this way, a Yoga or Zen snobbery could be encouraged, that is, some fad which would give a false twist to the whole matter. Further, it is asserted that Jungian psychology is exposed to the criticism of being a substitute for religion. Accusations of this kind are too general to be capable of a satisfactory examination in little space. It is all the more important to take note of Jung's own understanding of Eastern thought in its significance for the Westerner.

For a long time much has been thought and published

103

Rudolf Steiner.

about the differences between East and West. On the one hand are the accounts of those who do not examine what is specific in Eastern thought and, acting on the ancient device *"ex oriente lux"* (light comes from the East), make a pilgrimage to the Yoga teachers in India or to the Japanese priests of Zen Buddhism in order to fill with Asiatic spirituality the vacuum in the Westerner's mind and soul. The immense growth of relevant Western literature which does not always satisfy the demands of factual and scholarly criticism, and the numerous training centers that have arisen in Central Europe and America indicate the existence of such needs and show that, for example, the traditional Church teaching of the West has in fact lost its former leading role in spiritual and cultural matters. Syncretic tendencies mentioned by W. A. Visser 't Hooft—and for that matter by Jung too—do indeed exist. Our pluralistic secular age with its world-wide accent naturally encourages syncretism. The question is whether Jung can be blamed for this.

But, on the other hand, it cannot be overlooked that interest in Eastern thought is increasing and must be taken seriously. Among the first who, from the standpoint of Western and hence Christian thinking, had something illuminating to say about the polarity of East and West is Rudolf Steiner (1861-1925), who recognized the distinctive value of the Eastern outlook without thereby forgetting Western man's mission. Recently the French Jesuit Pierre Teilhard de Chardin (1881-1955), using the language of the theologian, the scientist, and the natural philosopher, has described the tendencies that suggest a global process of evolution which will converge in a single great human community.

Eastern thinkers of the stature of Sri Sarvepali Radhakrishnan (b. 1888), who was awarded the Peace Prize of the German Book Trade in 1961, are looking for that "Community of the Spirit" in which Eastern religiosity and Western thinking will find a place: "What we need are not creeds and programs, but the power of the spirit in the hearts of men, a power which will help us to subdue our passions of greed and selfishness and to organize the world which is at one with us in its wishes." Radhakrishnan's fellow countryman Sri Aurobindo (1872-1950), the creator of Integral Yoga, is optimistic about the East-West con-

Sri Aurobindo.

frontation when he says: "I do not see why there should be such an unbridgeable chasm. For there is in fact no fundamental difference in the spiritual life of the East and West. The differences always concern only the names, forms, and symbols. Or the emphasis is laid on one or another definite goal or on one or another side of psychological experience. And even in this respect the differences are often only arbitrarily supposed, whereas in truth they do not exist at all, or at any rate are not as great as seems to be the case."

Rudolf Steiner recognized such differences but not as the cause of any split there may be in the association of humanity, but rather in the sense of a complementary phenomenon. During a course of lectures on the opposing outlook of East and West, Steiner said on June 4, 1922, in Vienna: "In honoring the Orient for its spirituality, there is still something we need to be clear about: we must build up our own spirituality from the first step we have taken here in the West. We must so shape it, however, that we can achieve an understanding with any view that may exist on earth, especially old and venerable ones. This will be possible if, as Central and Western men, we come to understand that our philosophy of life has faults . . ."[114] However problematic it may be to compare philosophies of life, which are built up on different assumptions, as entities or in single pronouncements, points of comparison do become visible. Parallels can be drawn from case to case.

On two points Jung's attitude resembles—this is said with the necessary reserve—that of Steiner: Jung recognizes the need for completion of the Western mentality which is dominated by the intellect; he knows that East and West each represent half of the spiritual universe and that each of these standpoints, although contradictory of the other, has its psychological justification.[115] On the other hand, Jung does not conceal the fact that he is rooted in the tradition of Western Christianity, which makes it seem impossible to him that those forms of the Eastern spirit which he too admired can be taken over untried or be imitated by Westerners.

Before going on to deal with Jung's numerous pronouncements on general and special problems of Eastern spiritual life—his *Collected Works* contains contributions on the subject in the large volume *Psychology and Religion: West and East*—we need to ask what significance Jung attached to his study of this subject. Clarification is all the more desirable because the warnings quoted above about Jung's allegedly syncretic tendencies might be due to misunderstandings. In the Preface to the second edition of his commentary on the Chinese text edited by Richard Wilhelm, *The Secret of the Golden Flower*, Jung takes the opportunity to call attention to such "misunderstandings to which even well-informed readers of this book have succumbed. Not infrequently people thought that my purpose in publishing it was to put into the hands of the public a recipe for achieving happiness. In total misapprehension of all that I say in my commentary, these readers tried to imitate the 'method' described in the Chinese text. Let us hope that these representatives of spiritual profundity were few in number!''[116]

Jung sees the second misunderstanding in the opinion that, in his commentary, he had to some extent described his special therapeutic method ''which, it was said, consisted in my instilling Eastern ideas into my patients for therapeutic purposes. I do not believe there is anything in my commentary that lends itself to that sort of superstition. In any case such an opinion is altogether erroneous, and is based on the widespread view that psychology was invented for a specific purpose and is not an empirical science. To this category belongs the superficial as well as unintelligent opinion that the idea of the collective unconscious is 'metaphysical.' On the contrary, it is an empirical concept to be put alongside the concept of instinct, as is obvious to anyone who will read with some attention.''[117]

Jung has also refuted these misunderstandings in another connection. A significant example of his attitude towards Eastern spiritual life is to be found in the memorial speech which he delivered in Munich on May 10, 1930, on the occasion of a ceremony in honor of his friend and colleague Richard Wilhelm. These words, which will also be found in the Preface to the second edition of *The Secret of the Golden Flower*, express not only an appreciation of the great Sinologue to whom he attributes the rare charisma of ''spiritual motherliness,'' but Jung's relation to Eastern spiritual culture. That it may be understood, he demands the setting aside of existing prejudice and an unconditional

Schri Yantra.

readiness to accept this foreign spirituality, that is, an understanding surrender beyond all Christian resentment and all European arrogance. From experience he knew that all mediocre minds get lost because they either lose their roots or indulge in just as senseless a censoriousness.[118]

If Jung, referring to Wilhelm's cultural mission, said that he had brought "new light from the East," and that above all he had recognized how much the East had to give us to cure our distress, it is essential to consider in what context this statement was made: "The spiritual beggars of our day are unfortunately too inclined to appropriate the alms of the East and blindly to imitate its ways. There cannot be a sufficient warning against this danger, as Wilhelm also clearly felt. Spiritual Europe cannot be helped by mere sensation or a new titillation of the nerves. Rather, we must learn to earn in order to possess. What the East has to give us, we should take only as help in doing work we still have to perform. What is the use of the wisdom of the Upanishads, of the insights of Chinese Yoga, if we abandon our own foundations like dated misconceptions and settle on foreign shores like homeless, thieving pirates."[119]

Jung speaks just as plainly when he refers to the need to enlarge the European concept of knowledge, and then goes on: "We need a real three-dimensional life if we want to experience the wisdom of China as something living. Therefore we need first of all European wisdom about ourselves. Our way begins with European reality and not with yoga exercises which only deceive us about our own reality."[120]

Jung has a presentiment—it is 1930!—of the impending encounter: "The spirit of the East is really *ante portas.*" And he can already see two possibilities in the impending encounter between East and West. In it there could be a healing power or also a dangerous infection. The diagnostician leaves it therefore to his "patient's" capacity to decide what he can make of the possibilities.

Five years later, in February 1936, Jung published in the Calcutta review *Prabuddha Bharata* (in English) the essay entitled "Yoga and the West." If his joint studies with Richard Wilhelm led him previously to penetrate into the nature of Eastern traditions, this little treatise shows what, as a psychologist, he thinks of that Indian system for training body and mind. To begin with, Jung sees the development which has led Western man into conflict between faith and knowledge, between revelation and cognition. He finds there is "disorientation bordering on anarchy . . ."[121] During his historical development the European has moved so far away from his roots that his mind has finally split into faith and knowledge, just as every psychological exaggeration splits into its polarities."[122]

110

Yet Jung does not overlook the fact that there are certain facts concerning the history of consciousness to be revealed here and his disciple Erich Neumann (*Origins and History of Consciousness*) has undertaken this study. (Steiner pursued another path in writing *The Spiritual Guidance of Man and Humanity*.)

The result which Jung arrived at and which, significantly he published in an Indian review, runs as follows: "Because of the split in the Western mind, any adequate realization of the intentions of yoga is ruled out from the very beginning . . . The Indian knows not only his own nature but knows too to what degree he is himself. The European, on the other hand, has a science about nature and knows astonishingly little about his own nature, the nature within him."[123] Thus he calls for an image of man embracing the whole of reality. Elsewhere Jung looks at the psychic disposition which is quite different in the Easterner. And so he gives this advice: "I say to whom I can: 'Study yoga. You will learn a vast amount from it, but do not use it; for we Europeans are not made in such a way as to be able to use these methods directly. An Indian guru can explain everything to you and you can imitate everything. But do you know who is using yoga? In other words, do you know who you are and how you are made?' "[124]

Obviously Jung is not at all attacking yoga as such; he thinks that it is among the greatest creations of man. But he criticizes in a very decisive manner the adoption of yoga by a Westerner. "The spiritual development in the West has followed different paths than in the East and has therefore created conditions which represent thoroughly unfavorable ground for the application of yoga."[125]

Jung's thoughts culminate in a prophetic utterance: "The West will produce its own yoga in the course of

111

centuries and it will be created on the basis of Christianity."[126] This pronouncement too will have to be weighed if confusion with what has come to be regarded as "Yoga for Christians" or "Yoga for the West" is to be avoided. Jung is evidently thinking of more than a pragmatic application of Eastern practices for the Westerner. Although it is obvious that we take the author of *Yoga and the West* at his word, we must ask first what kind of yoga would be suitable for the Westerner in view of the nature of his constitution and his specific task for humanity and also because it was based on Christianity, and secondly whether there is a predisposition present.

This is an urgent question because of another problem which astonishingly enough was discussed in 1936 in the same essay. It is the problem of violence which has been growing in unprecedented proportions since the industrial revolution. What was written three years before the Second World War and nine years before Hiroshima and Nagasaki has acquired added significance for the present and the future. "The power of science and technology in Europe is so great and undisputed that there is almost no point in knowing what has been invented and what more can be done. The enormous possibilities are terrifying." Jung asks the ethical question: "Who uses this knowledge? Whose hands control this power? For the present, the state is a provisional means of protection; it apparently preserves the citizen from the enormous quantities of poisons and other infernal means of destruction which can be manufactured in thousands of tons at any time and in the shortest possible interval." And Jung goes on: "This knowledge has become so dangerous that the question becomes more and more urgent not what else could be done but what qualities the man should have who is put in charge of this 'knowledge' or how the frame of mind of

112

the Westerner could be changed so that he renounces his dreadful knowledge."[127] Jung certainly thinks that it is infinitely more important to deprive man, caught in the madness of his violence, of the illusion of his power than to "confirm him further in his error that he can do anything he wants."

But what is most striking in these words is his insight into the necessity for strengthening the powers of consciousness and increasing the inadequate moral force. What has to be done is not merely to make good the much-discussed cultural lag but, in addition, to activate those reserves of ethical understanding which modern man needs for overcoming the problems of his technology and civilization. Jung says therefore: "Western man does not need superiority over nature without and within. He has both to almost diabolical perfection. But what he does not have is the conscious recognition of his inferiority to nature around him and in him. What he ought to learn is that he cannot do what he wants. If he does not learn that, his own nature will destroy him. He does not know his own soul which is rebelling against him with suicidal intentions."[128]

Without seeking to underrate Jung's significance, one has nevertheless to state that, as a doctor, he confined himself chiefly to diagnosis. His psychology and psychotherapy does of course embrace, like no other method, facts from the widest range imaginable; but Jung does not feel called upon to be an innovator in cultural matters, or whatever one likes to call it. This self-restriction does him honor. But from a psychologist with his breadth of view, an investigation of the therapeutic and spiritual methods of training as practiced in the West could possibly have been desirable. Can this proposal ever have been put to him, for he would surely have agreed? Thus, of course, we

113

With a friend in Africa, 1925.

have from his pen psychological commentaries on texts from the field of Eastern religions, on the frequently mentioned *Golden Flower*, on the Tibetan *Book of the Great Liberation*, on the *Bardo Thödol*, on the *Tibetan Book of the Dead*; he has expressed an opinion on the psychology of Eastern meditation and written a series of detailed forewords, for example, to books by D. T. Suzuki, Heinrich Zimmer, and to the *I Ching*. Religious doctrines of the West, on the contrary—apart from late medieval alche-

In Egypt, 1926.

my—are mentioned briefly in a scarcely differentiated manner that is at times confusing for the non-expert, as, for example, the mass import of exotic religious systems, the religion of Abdul Bahai, the Sufutic sects, the Rama-krishna Mission, American Christian Science, the Anglo-Indian Theosophy of Helena Petrovna Blavatsky and Annie Besant, together with the Anthroposophy of Rudolf Steiner which leans consciously on the intellectual legacy of Central Europe.

In Jung's life and work, journeys overseas play a considerable role. During the Twenties he visited North Africa, then he went among the Pueblo Indians. ("Europe, our greatest problem, I only understand when I see where I as a European do not fit into the world."[129]) In 1925 he traveled through Kenya and Uganda. ("It was as if I were this moment returning to the land of my youth, and as if I knew that dark-skinned man who had been waiting for me for five thousand years. . . . I knew only that his world had been mine for countless millennia."[130])

In 1938 Jung accepted an invitation from the (British) Indian Government to take part in the celebrations marking the twenty-fifth anniversary of the foundation of Calcutta University. Apart from essays for reviews which were published in 1939 in the New York review *Asia*, there are notes about this in *Memories, Dreams, Reflections:* "India gave me my first experience of an alien, highly differentiated culture. Altogether different elements had been present during my Central African journey; culture had not predominated. As for North Africa, I never had the opportunity there to talk with a person capable of putting his culture into words. In India, however, I had the chance to speak with representatives of the Indian mentality, and to compare it with the Europeans. This was of the greatest significance."[131] Thus he met S. S. Subramanya Iyer, the guru of the Maharajah of Mysore. It is striking what special emphasis Jung lays on the statement that he had of course met numerous representatives of the cultural life of India but had studiously avoided all contact with so-called "holy men," the esoterics and spiritual leaders of India.

Henrich Zimmer, the great Indologist to whom Jung owes important insights into the nature of Indian culture, asked him if he had not at least been to see the great

116

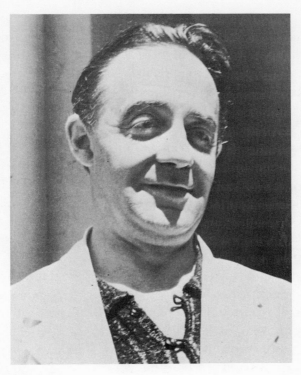

Heinrich Zimmer.

initiate, the Maharishi of Tiruvannamalai. Jung had to
admit that he had not. When in 1944 Jung wrote the
Introduction, "The Holy Men of India," to Henrich
Zimmer's last work *The Way to the Self: The Doctrine and
Life of the Indian Saint Sri Ramana Maharishi of Tiruvannamalai,* he said: "Perhaps I should have visited Sri
Ramana. Yet I fear that if I journeyed to India a second
time to make up for my omission, it would fare with me
just the same: I simply could not, despite the uniqueness
of the occasion, bring myself to visit this undoubtedly
distinguished man personally."[132] Why was that so? Jung
thought that this "uniqueness" was typical, that it could
be met with again in many forms in the daily life of India.

It could only claim uniqueness from the point of view of the European. "Therefore it was not necessary to seek him out. I saw him all over India, in the pictures of Ramakrishna, in Ramakrishna's disciples, in Buddhist monks, in innumerable other figures of the daily Indian scene, and the words of his wisdom are the *sous-entendu* of India's spiritual life."[133]

Jung has many appreciative things to say about Ramana and the Indians who are advanced in spiritual maturity. "I in no way underestimate the significant figure of the Indian saint but certainly do not credit myself with the ability to form an estimate of him as an isolated phenomenon."[134] The last reason for this reserve is given in that reference to the spiritual roots of the psyche of Western man when Jung says in this connection: "I would have felt it as a theft had I attempted to learn from the holy men and to accept their truth for myself. Their wisdom belongs to them and I have only what comes out of myself. Nor in Europe can I make any borrowings from the East, but must shape my life out of myself."[135] On the occasion of his journey to India, Jung expressed the need to shape his life out of himself by continuing his alchemical studies, to which end he took with him the compendium *Theatrum Chemicum* dating from the year 1602. He studied the book "from beginning to end. Thus it was that this material belonging to the fundamental strata of European thought was constantly counterpointed by my impressions of a foreign mentality and culture. Both had emerged from original psychic experiences of the unconscious, and therefore had produced the same, similar, or at least comparable insights."[136]

We seem to have a statement of what Indian and Eastern spiritual life meant to Jung in the description and interpretation of a dream he had towards the end of his stay in

118

India which had been so rich in impressions. The dream imagery itself has nothing to do with the traditions of the country which he had now come to know from firsthand experience but relates to a central piece of Western esotericism, the Holy Grail. "Imperiously, the dream wiped away all the intense impressions of India and swept me back to the too-long-neglected concerns of the Occident, which had formerly been expressed in the quest for the Holy Grail as well as in the search for the philosophers' stone. I was taken out of the world of India, and reminded that India was not my task, but only a part of the way—admittedly a significant one—which should carry me closer to my goal. It was as though the dream were asking me, "What are you doing in India? Rather seek for yourself and your fellows the healing vessel, the *servator mundi*, which you urgently need. For your state is perilous; you are all in imminent danger of destroying all that centuries have built up."[137]

India had of course dug its traces into Jung, as he confesses. However, India's spirituality was for him not the goal but at best a stop along the way—the way of Western man.

An important principle resulted from his study of the mind of the East. It is what Jung later elaborated and called "synchronicity" or the "synchronistic principle." He came upon this phenomenon when working on the Chinese book of oracles, the *I Ching*: "The function on which the practice of I Ching is based . . . is, as far as can be seen, in the sharpest contradiction to our Western world outlook with its scientific causality."[138] For Jung, the form of thinking present in the *I Ching* was of great significance because the experiences of his psychological practice had been causing him to look for a suitable principle which would explain certain psychic phenomena.

"For I found at first that there were psychological parallel phenomena that simply could not be related to one another causally but must be connected as events in some other way. This connection seemed essentially to exist in the fact of relative simultaneousness, hence the expression 'synchronistic.' For it seems as if time is anything but an abstract notion, but rather a concrete continuum which contains qualities or basic conditions that can manifest themselves in relative simultaneousness in different places in a parallelism that cannot be explained causally, as, for example, in cases of the simultaneous appearance of identical thoughts, symbols, or psychic states."[139]

Jung hesitated a long time before, at the Eranos Conference in 1951, he spoke about synchronicity and then, in the volume *Interpretation of Nature and the Psyche*, co-authored with Wolfgang Pauli, presented a detailed account of "Synchronicity as an Acausal Connecting Principle." There he writes: "Synchronicity is no more baffling or mysterious than the discontinuities of physics. It is only the ingrained belief in the sovereign power of causality that creates intellectual difficulties and makes it appear unthinkable that causeless events exist or could ever occur. But if they do, then we must regard them as 'creative acts,' as the continuous creation of a pattern that exists from all eternity, repeats itself sporadically, and is not derivable from any known antecedents . . . Meaningful coincidences are thinkable as pure chance. But the more they multiply and the greater and more exact the correspondence is, the more their probability sinks and their unthinkability increases, until they can no longer be regarded as pure chance but, for lack of a causal explanation, have to be thought of as meaningful arrangements . . ."[140]

For these and similar reasons, Jung derived the necessity for introducing along with space, time, and causality a category "which comprises not only the characterization of synchronicity phenomena as a special class of natural events, but also the contingent as, on the one hand, something general and present from time immemorial, and, on the other, as the sum of many individual acts of creation taking place in time."[141] (The difficulties of the questions connected with the problem of synchronicity require a detailed study of the relevant literature, which is impossible in this limited space.)

Just as modern physics broke open the framework of the scientific view of the world which had been valid up to then, and made fluid those natural laws which had been regarded as absolute, Jung's contributions throw light on a new and wider understanding of reality.

PSYCHOTHERAPY

Carl Gustav Jung began as a psychiatrist and psychotherapist, although the foundations for what today is understood by those words had still to be created—decisively, by Jung himself. When, in 1957, in the German edition of the *Collected Works*, the sixteenth volume, *The Practice of Psychotherapy*, was placed at the beginning, the octogenarian wished to approve this step. To his publishers—Marianne Niehus-Jung, Lena Hurwitz and Franz N. Riklin were then in charge—he expressed his agreement and gratitude: "By your action you show your understanding for the fact that my contribution to knowledge of the soul rests on practical experience with human beings. It is in fact a medical endeavor to gain psychologi-

121

cal understanding of mental suffering which, in more than fifty years of psychotherapeutic practice, has led me to all my later discoveries and conclusions and, on the other hand, has caused me to check and modify my insights again in direct experience."[142]

But how are works dealing with psychotherapeutic practice to be associated with investigations of a more historical nature? In the Preface to this volume Jung calls attention to the fact that historical reflection and psychotherapeutic practice are only seemingly incommensurable magnitudes. Rather does it become repeatedly clear in the treatment of a patient "how eminently historical mental behavior is. Not only must the psychotherapist find out all about the personal biography of his patient but also all about the intellectual assumptions of the intellectual world around him, whether far or near, where traditional and ideological influences come in and often play a decisive role." And he adds that no psychiatrist will therefore be spared the task of dealing with the symbolism of dream language. And exactly for that reason knowledge is necessary which goes far beyond academic natural science and medicine. Jung offers in his own person the best proof of this necessity.

From what has been said it follows quite automatically that "Contributions to the Problem of Psychotherapy and the Psychology of the Transference" (as the subtitle has it) can also not be contrasted with books whose contents deal chiefly with "historical" subjects.

Jung often took the opportunity, both through the spoken and the written word, at medical congresses, in public lectures and press releases, to present the fundamental and practical side of psychotherapeutic work. This was all the more necessary because the endeavors related to psychotherapy only gradually won recognition from the academic world and the public. On the occasion of a lecture on "Some Aspects of Modern Psychotherapy," which was to be delivered at the Congress of Public Health in 1929 in Zurich, Jung put forward the following for consideration: "Psychotherapy and modern psychology have for the present remained individual experiments and ventures and have hitherto found little or no general application. Its application is left entirely to the personal initiative of the individual doctors and they are not even supported by the universities. And yet the problems of modern psychology have aroused such great interest that the little official recognition which they receive bears no relation to it . . . Medical psychology is still pioneering work."[143]

There was an additional difficulty because the young movement inaugurated essentially by Freud and Breuer

The ten stages of life. An animal is allotted to each age, which is personified by a human figure. Death stands as a symbol of mortality behind the central figure, the fifty-year-old man. Engraving by Jörg Breu the Younger, about 1530.

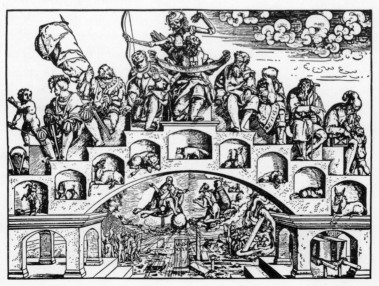

split up too soon into "schools" with seemingly contrary starting points, not to mention the shock which Freud's theory of sex administered and had linked once for all with the concept of psychoanalysis. Undoubtedly Jung had to do a great deal of pioneering work. It included the role of mediator between the different doctrines: "I always needed to take many kinds of opinions together. I could never fail in the long run to see the rightness of diverging opinions,[144] Jung said in a report to the Congress of the German Psychotherapeutic Association in 1929. As Jung pointed out in connection with his typology, differing and even opposite positions and opinions are usually connected with corresponding basic psychic facts in the person concerned. The diagnostician recognizes something from which the therapist has to draw practical conclusions.

What does Jung actually understand by psychotherapy? What principles come into play, what are the objectives, what means are employed to attain them?

To begin with, it is important to note that psychotherapy as Jung understands it is not a simple method. Older procedures, the so-called method of suggestion, had to be given up. The patient could not be degraded to the level of a passive object but had to be drawn into a "dialectical procedure," into a process in which there was a fruitful exchange between doctor and patient calling for the patient's cooperation. (We shall later see that Jung's work was closely criticized by Martin Buber and some of Jung's disciples because his dialectical procedure did not amount to a full dialogue technique.)

The relationship between doctor and patient is formulated as follows: "A person is a psychic system which, when it affects another person, enters into a reciprocal reaction with another psychic system."[145] However technical this definition of Jung's, which he felt to be "most modern," may sound, it is intelligible from his standpoint. He is concerned with making use of his insight into a person's psychic or typological assumpions at a given moment. They are expressed in the doctor-patient relationship. In contrast to earlier suggestion therapy, the individual is taken seriously. Hence great demands are made on the therapist. "He is no longer the agent of treatment but a fellow participant in a process of individual development."[146] Thus qualities are demanded which are commensurate with the risk in every thorough psychotherapeutic course of treatment. And so Jung was one of the first to demand that an analyst should himself have been analyzed. He too may have complexes which may act as blind spots in diagnosis and have serious consequences in the therapy. Jung therefore states this principle: "The patient's treatment begins with the doctor, so to speak. Only if the doctor knows how to cope with himself and his own problems will he be able to teach the patient to do the same."[147]

A problem of a special nature is represented by transference, to the importance of which Freud had called attention at an early date. Jung knew that in analytical practice it is almost impossible for the personal relationship between doctor and patient not to play a large part, at least from time to time. And under certain circumstances, a partly conscious, partly unconscious identification of doctor and patient may arise. The therapist must be prepared for such possibilities. That he should have an accurate knowledge of the relevant methods is an obvious assumption of all he does, although the dialectical or dialogue situation of the psychotherapeutic course of treatment does not permit a prepared plan of treatment to be stated: "I am often asked about my psychotherapeutic or analytic

The soul as guide leading the way. Watercolor illustration by William Blake for Dante's *Purgatorio*, Canto IV.

method. I cannot reply unequivocally to the question. Therapy is different in every case. When a doctor tells me that he adheres strictly to this or that method, I have my doubts about his therapeutic effect . . . Psychotherapy and analysis are as varied as are human individuals . . . Universal rules can be postulated only with a grain of salt. A psychological truth is valid only if it can be reversed. A solution which would be out of the question for me may be just the right one for someone else."[148]

As for the objective of psychotherapy Jung takes the view that it can be marked out on a scientific basis in free research. Accordingly, the psychotherapist's purpose is "to train his patient to independence of being and to moral freedom in conformity with knowledge which is the result of unprejudiced research."[149] The context in which these words were spoken during a lecture in 1941 clearly indicates that psychotherapy must not be falsified by ideological penetration or state guidance. Jung does not accept the objection that the individual has to be subordinated to the interests of the State. As one who has observed as a psychologist the politico-social developments in the first half of the twentieth century, he is aware of the seductive power which society can exert when the State makes totalitarian claims and enforces them by the use of the most brutal means. These investigations have been recorded in his *Essays on Contemporary Events.* Jung therefore says that it is the objective of therapy to become one with oneself and at the same time with humanity. This process of maturing in its final form he calls "individuation." For Jung, there is a true community where this process leading to the independence of the individual is affirmed in freedom. And Jung knows on the other hand: "Where there is no such community, the independent individual with a foundation of his own cannot thrive."[150]

Just as Jung searches for a balance between what is individual and the forces of society, so he calls for a balance between joy and sorrow. Life can only find wholeness and fulfillment when the sorrow and pain which fate bring are accepted: "Therefore the principal aim of psychotherapy is not to transport the patient to an impos-

127

sible state of happiness, but to help him acquire steadfastness and philosophic patience in face of suffering.''[151] Behind this Stoic-sounding attitude a clear yes is said to what the world can offer, a yes which—in contrast to the Oriental attitude to life—can only be spoken from a Christian standpoint. And this is what characterizes Jung's approach as a therapist.

This outlook put the psychiatrist's work, which is often tedious and laborious, into a great context. The practical work consists admittedly of small and even very tiny steps aimed at illuminating what comes from the unconscious in a form which is at first incomprehensible. Freud had once begun with the watchword "making conscious the causes" of faulty psychic development. After suggestive or hypnotic treatment there had come one in which Freud's theory of repression could be used. According to this theory, the ego (as the conscious part of the psychic apparatus) relegates contents which are felt as distressing to the unconscious, that is to say, represses them by consigning them to the id. "The theory of repression took far more account of the fact that typical neuroses are, properly speaking, developmental disturbances. Freud put it that the disturbance was due to the repression of infantile sexual impulses and tendencies which were thereby made unconscious.''[152] In investigating the dream, which is "our favorite object of study" (Freud), the doctor has to look for these facts in the patient. With his epoch-making work *The Interpretation of Dreams* (1900), Freud cleared the way for modern psychotherapy to do this.

Carl Gustav Jung always spoke highly of this fact, although a comparison shows that he could not agree everywhere with the author of *The Interpretaion of Dreams*, either in practical or theoretical matters. Apart from the above-mentioned ideological assumptions of Freud, Jung gives the patient's attitude precedence over Freud's attempt to find causes: "The task of psychotherapy is to correct the conscious attitude and not to go chasing after infantile memories."[153] Jung does of course recognize that there cannot be one without the other, but he places the main emphasis on the observation of the conscious attitude of the patient. The reason he gives is the neurotic's tendency to indulge in memories and self-pity: "Very often his neurosis consists precisely in his hanging back and constantly excusing himself on account of his past."[154] We have already mentioned that, in addition, Jung attaches value to the active cooperation of the patient, even in examining dreams.

In addition to the difference of emphasis, there is the divergence in the interpretation of psychic phenomena, especially as concerns dreams. In one of his last works, which remained unfinished (*Outline of Psychoanalysis*, begun in 1938), Freud sketched once again his method of dream interpretation: "We can find our way towards understanding (or 'interpreting') dreams, if we assume that what we recollect as the dream after we have woken up is not the true dream process but only a façade behind which that process lies concealed."[155] This conception is characteristic of Freud's starting point. He distinguishes therefore "manifest" dream material from "latent" dream thoughts. Dream work consists accordingly in making visible the evident dream content out of the dream thought concealed behind a kind of façade. The unconscious is expressed only indirectly in the dream, especially since a "censor" produces distortion. The dream, according to Freud, gives expression to a repressed wish and so corresponds to a suppressed wish-fulfillment. By an appropriate method, namely that developed by Freud, the dream can be "interpreted," largely causally. In *Introductory Lectures on Psychoanalysis* (1916/1917), Freud could actually say that the symbolism appearing in the dream allowed the psychoanalyst in certain circumstances to interpret a dream without interrogating the dreamer.

With Jung it is different. He can scarcely be credited with such self-confidence concerning the application of a method. This is not because he is less aware of his own worth but because of his own different approach. Jung credited Freud with bold efforts to illuminate dream psychology with the aid of points of view taken from psychopathology, but, while admiring his bold attempt, could neither agree with his methods nor with his results.[156]

Even the question about what a dream is receives a different answer from Jung. For Jung the dream is an underground reflection of the psyche and its meaning can be uncovered empirically. From experience he knows that, "if one meditates long enough and thoroughly enough on a dream, carrying it about with one and turning

The nocturnal voyage: Joseph in the well; burial of Christ; Jonah swallowed by the whale. Illustrations from the *Biblia Pauperum*, German edition of 1471.

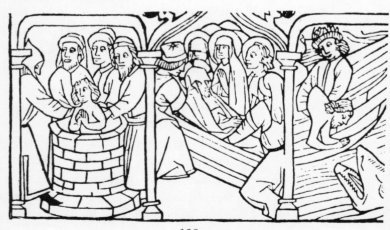

it over now and again, something can usually be made of it."[157] But what is made of it is not hidden behind a "façade." The neurotic, Jung believes, does have something disagreeable to cover up. But can that be said in general of every dreamer? Jung doubted whether it could be assumed that a dream was something other than it appeared to be. After referring to the Talmud, the authors of which, belonging to antiquity, had uncommon experience of dreams, Jung sets against Freud's thesis the antithesis: "I take the dream for what it is."[158] In view of the difficult and complicated thing which a dream is, giving difficulty even to an experienced depth psychologist, he does not venture to credit the unconscious with a tendency to deceive. *Allgemeine Gesichtspunkte* (*General Viewpoint*), published in 1928, contains the definition: "The dream is a psychic structure which is unlike that of other contents of consciousness because, so far as we can judge from their form and meaning, they do not show the continuity of development typical of conscious contents."[159] And for Jung the dream is also a natural event. He can see no reason why it should be a crafty device "to lead us astray."[160] After all, neurotics are not the only people who dream. And he adds that nature is often obscure and opaque, but it is not cunning like a human being, so, therefore, one must suppose that a dream is exactly what it is supposed to be, neither more nor less.[161]

As for the question of the continuity of the dream, which has been touched upon, Jung asserts that there is a continuity backwards and forwards. This brings up an important problem of interpretation, a further point where the Freudian view with its chiefly causal orientation is contradicted. Jung enriches the causal view by considering the end. He asks to what purpose, as well as why, and remarks at the same time: "Considering a dream from the

131

standpoint of finality, which I contrast with the causal standpoint of Freud, does not—as I would expressly like to emphasize—involve a denial of the dream's causes, but rather a different interpretation of the associative material gathered round the dream.''[162]

From this there obviously arise consequences for the interpretation of dreams in general. It does not remain bound to one or more rigid premises or to a uniform symbolic significance. Instead of only one possible meaning, the alternatives are open in the sense of genuine symbols in several dimensions. Jung believed that a symbol was only alive when it was full of significance.[163]

But what is Jung's practical technique?

"When, therefore, we seek a psychological explanation of a dream, we must first know what were the preceding experiences out of which it is composed.''[164] Every single part of the dream picture has to be referred to any earlier experiences. What has been dreamed is never a separate thing, but rather has to be taken in its context. Other dreams occurring at the same period of time, especially dream series, need to be taken with it. As is well known, they play an extremely important role in Jung's creative work. Related motifs can appear in the image language and possibly make the interpretation easier. From this or from a sudden change of motifs appropriate conclusions can be drawn. Awareness of the dreamer's momentary state of consciousness is likewise important. The same applies to the philosophical, religious, and moral convictions of consciousness. It is Jung's opinion that all dreams compensate the conscious content at the moment, even when this compensating function is not always clearly to be seen. "It is therefore not suprising that religious compensations play a great role in dreams.''[165] Jung finds an explanation for this need for compensation in the prevailing materialistic and atheistic or non-religious attitude of modern man. In addition to this, Jung considers Freud's conception of the dream function as wish fulfillment too narrow.

The distinction between a "manifest dream content" and a "latent dream thought" does not apply to Jung. The Jungian position is characterized by another differentiation which specially affects interpretation. A dream can take place on the "subject" or on the "object" level. Dream interpretation on the "object level" means that the dreamer's experiences deal with the objects, people, and things in the world around him. Dream interpretation on the "subject level" means that the same dream images refer to the dreamer and portray his frame of mind; they provide a backwards view of the past or a warning by calling attention to what may possibly be going to happen. Seen in this way all dream creation is "subjective, and a dream is a theater in which the dreamer is himself the scene, the player, the prompter, the producer, the author, the public, and the critic. This simple truth forms the basis for a conception of the dream's meaning which I have called 'interpretation on the subjective level.' Such an interpretation, as the term implies, conceives all the figures in the dream as personified features of the dreamer's own personality."[166] Of course, it has to be carefully considered when the attempt at interpretation is made, whether the subject level or object level will lead to the goal, i.e., "whether the image is reproduced for its subjective or for its objective significance."[167]

Using an abundance of examples from his own practice, in which he said himself that he often analyzed more than a thousand dreams in a year, Jung has presented in his books the foundations and methodical possibilities of dream interpretation as developed by him. It only remains to be added that the purposefulness of Jungian interpretative endeavors receives further emphasis by the introduction of the end-point of view. These endeavors are at the service of psychotherapy and here again at the service of the real goal, which is that of individuation. The process of individuation is expressed in the most diverse symbols, which are often related to conceptions of folklore, Gnosticism, alchemy, and shamanism. Since these materials can

Night voyage of Hercules in the cup of the sun. Base of an Attic vase of the fifth century B.C. Etruscan Museum, Vatican.

recur in dream series—Jung has demonstrated this in a most impressive manner in his work—the process of becoming whole, of being cured, can be followed interpretatively in the dream happenings. "When material of this kind is adduced for comparison, the exposition fairly swarms with 'exotic' and 'far-fetched' proofs, and anyone who merely skims through a book instead of reading it can easily succumb to the illusion that he is confronted with a Gnostic system. In reality, however, individuation is an expression of that biological process— simple or complicated as the case may be—by which every living thing becomes what it was destined to become from the beginning."[168]

If dream symbols represent, as it were, bridges linking the conscious and the unconscious, a comprehensive and accurate knowledge of them is indispensable for the analyst. On the other hand, the Jungian analyst is saved from the self-assurance that the mere knowledge of symbols—which Jung so notably possessed—itself represents a kind of key to the unconscious with the help of which one can work without it being necessary to question the dreamer, as Freud said. What becomes important here is the demand for cooperation through the dialogue of doctor and patient. The doctor becomes a helper to achieve the goal expressed by "become what thou art." In the middle of this healing process a "way of healing" is prepared. (Jung consciously avoids this designation. As a Westerner he sees the way of healing in Christianity. He has outspokenly rejected any religious claims. For, after all, he knows much too well that the way of individuation can be threatened by considerable obstacles and dangers. For this reason Jung is free from the suspicion of having gone beyond his medical field of competence.) Jung's ecclesiastical and theological critics did, however, express the fear that psychotherapy was becoming one of the many substitute religions of modern secularism.

Apart from the fact that every honest endeavor which is commendable because of its approach can be perverted or caricatured by ill-advised imitators and critics, their results should not be confused with what was originally intended. As regards this point, it is very certain that, during the course of therapeutic treatment, buried religious activity can be brought to light and revived. In the ciphers of the dream images it is possible to hear "God's forgotten language," as the Protestant theologian John A. Sandford has shown in his book of the same name. We have already said that Jung was not tempted to support any confessional Church or even to succumb to confessionalism. He remained a doctor and a healer, but in a pre-eminent sense of course.

Considered in this way, Jung's psychotherapy is more than one analytical procedure among others, although its creator was concerned to show a critical respect for scientific assumptions. In her thoughtful Introduction, Jolande Jacobi has demonstrated to what extent Jung's psychology does indeed represent a "way of healing." As she sees it, the element of experience is again stressed. Psychotherapy can only inadequately be described. To be deeply involved, to have personal experience and suffering is an essential part. That is why Jolande Jacobi writes: "Jung's psychotherapy is a '*Heilsweg*,' a 'way of healing' in both meanings of the German term, which signifies at the same time 'healing' and 'salvation.' It has all the requisites for 'healing' a person from his psychic and therewith connected psychogenic sufferings. It has all the instruments for removing the most complicated developments of mental disease. But besides this it knows the way and has the means to lead the individual to his own 'healing'

136

(*Heil*), to that knowledge and perfection of his own personality which has ever been the aim and goal of all spiritual striving. This way is, from its very nature, beyond all abstract exposition. Theoretic conceptions and explanations are adequate only up to a certain point for the comprehension of Jung's system of thought, for in order to understand it completely, one must have experienced its vital working on oneself. To this one can only refer, as to every happening that essentially influences man."[169] It would not be out of keeping with Jung's work to want to keep open that character which his psychotherapy has as tool and "way" in order to meet the uncontrollable, that which fate has in store for man, and, finally, that which, in the religious sense, comes from the realm of grace. Healing and salvation come together here.

PROBLEMS OF OUR TIME

Jung did not confine himself to illuminating psychic problems of the individual and to using for this purpose archaic image contents as a means of "amplification." Contemporary events, the fate of nations, concerned him as a doctor in just the same way. And because he was concerned about wholeness, that the psyche should become whole, he could not remain indifferent to biological, politico-social, and contemporary factors in the framework of all that was happening. "We are living in times of great disruption: political passions are aflame, internal upheavals have brought nations to the brink of chaos, and the very foundations of our *Weltanschauung* are shattered. This critical state of things has such a tremendous in-

Bollingen, about 1955.

fluence on the psychic life of the individual that the doctor
is bound to follow its effect on the individual psyche with
more than usual attention. The storm of actual events does
not only sweep down upon him from the great world
outside; he feels the violence of its impact even in the
quiet of his consulting room and in the privacy of the

medical consultation." The psychiatrist, therefore, cannot withdraw to mere scientific work or even succumb to a mysticism which is remote from the present and hostile to reality, "but must constantly descend into the arena of world events, in order to join in the battle of conflicting passions and opinions."[170]

These lines are to be found in the preface to the small volume of *Essays on Contemporary Events* (1946). There are three fairly short essays belonging to the time of National Socialism, and one essay which was composed shortly after the catastrophe of the Second World War. These essays are also of great significance for forming an estimate of Jung's own attitude to National Socialism and so indirectly to National Socialistic anti-Semitism, since the rumor had been spread that Jung, who, as an "Aryan," had once broken with the "Jew" Freud, had certain sympathies for the rulers of the Third Reich and had expressed his antipathy for things Jewish. Jung had indeed said controversial things which a biographer cannot pass by in silence, but Jung was never a Nazi or an anti-Semite. That is also a fact which emerges from the essays that were written as a direct reaction to contemporary events.

In February 1933, that is, a few days after Hitler took over power on January 30, 1933, Jung delivered lectures in Cologne and Essen in which he made quite clear his views on the situation in Germany. He spoke of a "compensatory regression to the collective man," which, he said, had come about as the necessary consequence of an exaggerated individualistic trend. "Collective man is threatening to suffocate the individual, the very individual who is absolutely indispensable, for it is on his sense of responsibility that every human achievement is ultimately founded. The crowd in itself is always anonymous and irresponsible. So-called '*Führers*' are the inevitable symp-

139

toms of a mass movement. The true leaders of men are always those who carry themselves, and relieve the crowd at least of their own weight, in that they consciously do not allow themselves to be carried away by the blind laws of nature that move the masses."[171]

In 1936 the *Neue Schweizer Rundschau* printed Jung's essay "*Wotan.*" The author saw in this old Germanic god of storm and frenzy a figure "who releases passions and the lust of war, moreover he is a paramount magician and a conjurer who is versed in every occult secret."[172] Jung interprets him as an archetype who, "as an autonomous psychic factor, produces effects in the collective life of the people and thus also reveals his own character."[173] Jung observed how the national god, and not only in Germany, had attacked Christianity in a menacing fashion, and how the individual found it impossible to resist Wotan's on-rush. Seen from this angle, the following comment by Jung is worth attention: "We, who stand outside, judge the Germans as if they were responsible, active agents, but perhaps we should be nearer the truth if we were also to regard them as victims."[174] This opinion is not meant in any way as an excuse; for when, in 1945, Jung, with a heavy heart, decided to write *After the Catastrophe,* the Swiss doctor diagnosed not only a kind of collective hysteria which had attacked Germany, and indeed all Europe, but he also spoke of a collective guilt, in the psychological sense, common to the Germans, the Europeans, and the Christian Church.[175]

If today one reads the notes written in the years when the Hitler régime had still to reach the zenith of its power, one can hardly fail to see in Jung's conclusions signs of an almost prophetic clairvoyance. He wrote that "National Socialism would not be the last word. Things must be concealed in the background which we cannot imagine as yet, but we can expect them to appear in the course of the next years [i.e., after 1936] or decades. Wotan's awakening is a sort of stepping back or reaching back. The river has been dammed up and has broken into its original channel. But the dam will not last forever."[176]

If Jung said or did anything questionable during the time of the Third Reich, which might have led Ernst Bloch, for example, to abuse the Swiss psychiatrist as a "psychoanalyst foaming with fascism" (in *Das Prinzip Hoffnung,* Frankfurt am Main, 1959, p. 65), Aniela Jaffé's book *Aus Leben und Werkstatt von C. G. Jung (From the Life and Workshop of C. G. Jung)* clarifies his actions by presenting the facts in their context. Miss Jaffé points out, for example, that one of Jung's first official actions as President of the Allgemeine Ärztliche Gesellschaft für Psychotherapie was to enact a regulation on behalf of his Jewish colleagues in Germany. "His active support for the Jews, however, did not prevent him as a psychologist from stressing the difference between Jewish and non-Jewish psychology." Then there were false and offensive remarks about Jewry and Jewishness. The ardent disciple and biographer of Jung makes no attempt to gloss over anything when she continues: "The fact that Jung spoke out at the very moment when the Jews' existence was threatened, and placed the psychological-racist differences on the scientific program of the International Society was a serious blunder." But it is a fact that, when the dreadful background of the National Socialist régime became known, whose roots the depth psychologist must surely have known about earlier, as evidenced by the above quotations, Jung subjected his ambiguous attitude to unsparing criticism. Aniela Jaffé, who can point to a letter from Professor Gerschon G. Scholem, Jerusalem, indicating that there had been a reconcillation between Leo

141

Baeck and Carl Gustav Jung, reaches the conclusion: "In retrospect his mistakes and errors at that time can be seen to fit into his life and work without diminishing the greatness of his personality. In the words of Jungian psychology one could say that the shadow became manifest which is in everyone as an archetype and is often all the darker when a brighter light comes from the personality. Jung has given too much to the world and to mankind

Jung the artisan, Bollingen, about 1955.

for his shadow ever to put in question his intellectual significance and his human greatness."[177]

Two further examples which are evidence of Jung's active participation in contemporary events are worthy of mention: his answer to the controversial question of "flying saucers," and, secondly, his *Answer to Job,* in which the depth psychologist takes up his position on the Marian dogma in the year 1950.

"Flying saucers," as "UFOs" (Unidentified Flying Objects) have been called, have fired the imagination of many contemporaries, not least that of authors of science fiction. Together with serious investigations of the subject, there is a flood of writing hardly worth mentioning. People therefore listened when in 1958 Jung came into the discussion with his book *Ein Moderner Mythus. Von Dingen, die am Himmel gesehen werden (Et, A Modern Myth. Things Seen in the Sky).* This work shows how attentively Jung has studied the phenomena and searched through all the relevant literature.

Is there then anything real about UFOs or are they an illusion of the senses? Jung replies that there is a link between UFOs and latent psychic contents. He finds it unlikely that there are any unknown meteoric phenomena, "since the behavior of the objects in no way gives rise to the impression that there is any physical process to be interpreted. The movements of the objects betray freakishness and psychic reference, e.g., evasion and flight, perhaps even aggression and/or defense." In his opinion, acceleration, angle of direction, and degrees of heat produced are such that no earthly creature could stand them. What emerges are clearly realities, although here too as a psychologist he confines himself basically to the relations between UFOs and the psyche by explaining them as a collective vision or as a visionary rumor whose

143

symbolic significance he interprets. His conclusion is as follows: "For what we have here is nothing less than two possibilities: either psychic projections are reflecting a radar echo [this has been established with UFOs], or, on the other hand, the appearance of real bodies has given rise to mythological projections."[178] This is not enough. In his interpretation of the phenomena Jung becomes even more concrete by crediting the UFOs with apocalyptic relevance: "It is not arrogance but my medical conscience telling me to do my duty to prepare the few to whom I can make myself heard that events are in store for mankind which correspond to the end of an aeon . . . There are, seemingly, changes in the constellation of the psychic dominants, the archetypes, the "gods," which cause or accompany secular transformations of the collective psyche . . . I am, frankly speaking, worried about the lot of those who will be caught unprepared by events and be unsuspectingly delivered up to their incomprehensibility."

In any case, Jung allows of no doubt regarding the threatening nature of the world situation. Both the psychic condition of the individual and that of the whole of mankind are involved. Whatever one may think of the details of Jung's pronouncements (there were heated discussions about the book), one thing is certain: in *A Modern Myth* the psychologist is provocative—but on important matters. The Christian theologian, for example, will be stimulated to meditate afresh on the mighty and usually rarely accessible chapters of eschatology, that is, of dogmatic doctrine about future things and the Second Coming of Christ. Ancient esoteric thought and modern intellectualism (for instance, that of Rudolf Steiner) throw light on what Jung had to say. Finally, as an expert on esoteric astrology, Jung knows that with the entry of spring into Aquarius a great change was to be expected. All this, Jung thought, suggested a turning point in the world's affairs in respect to which, for example, the phenomena of history on the surface could be regarded as symptoms of an activity stirring behind the scenes, the nature and purpose of which has to be grasped by cognition.

Jung's attitude to contemporary events, as it is reflected in *Answer to Job* (1952), is of a different nature. Here the psychologist deals with areas which seem to be reserved for the theologian, if not for the Gnostic or mystic in particular. This book can be considered as one of the most personal and passionate that Jung has written. He describes how Job, afflicted by fate or, more precisely, by the wrath of Yahweh, and bitterly reproached by his friends, comes to recognize the antinomy of God, that is, the opposites in the divine nature with which Jung dealt again and again. Jung sees good and evil, love and hate, the divine and the satanic united in Yahweh. This divine darkness, in Jung's view, disperses in the Old Testament in the Book of Job, thereby making it a "landmark in the long historical development of a divine drama."[179] "Job realizes God's inner antinomy and in the light of this realization his knowledge attains a divine numinosity."[180] This process of realization which Job goes through so painfully places him "morally higher than Yahweh. In this respect the creature has surpassed the creator . . . Yahweh must become man precisely because he has done man a wrong . . . Because his creature has surpassed him, he must regenerate himself."[181]

It is not necessary to stress that these reflections take Jung a very long way from the canons of Church dogma. Nor will the attentive reader fail to notice those lines in the book where the author, who is as unreservedly frank as he is committed, credits the God of the Old Testament and the God of the New Testament Gospel according to Saint John with remarks closely bordering on cynicism and blasphemy, although the context refutes this suspicion. What then is the goal and purpose of *Answer to Job?* Jung's chief concern is to call attention to the religious problem of Job: "The aim of my book is to trace the historical development of this problem since the time of Job down through the centuries to the most recent symbolic events." The problem of the tension of opposites contained in God had engaged Jung's attention for many years. He confesses: "I was caught by the urgency and deep significance of the problem and could not get away from it. Thus I was forced to take up the whole problem, and I did this by describing a personal experience which was accompanied by subjective emotions. I chose this form deliberately because I wanted to avoid the impression that I had intended to proclaim an 'eternal truth.' The book does not set out to be anything but the questioning voice of a single person who hopes or expects to meet with a thoughtful reception from his readers."[182]

No doubt Jung met with this thoughtful reception and even with contradiction, above all at that place in the book where he speaks about the latest Marian dogma of the Roman Catholic Church (the Assumption of Mary). Primal religious conceptions of the feminine element in the Godhead, designated in Jewish-Christian tradition as "Sophia" or as the "wisdom of God," take on a contemporary significance for Jung. The religions of antiquity were familiar with the mystery of the heavenly nuptials (*Hieros Gamos*), the union of a divine male principle with a divine female principle as represented in the image of the hermaphrodite or the androgyne.

146

The Virgin Mary as personification of the firmament. From the *Speculum humanae Salvationis,* fifteenth century, Vatican.

As the son of a Protestant pastor, Jung feels all the more clearly the result of an historical process of repression in the course of which the Sophia element was actually denied officially, especially by Protestant theory and the Evangelical Church. Only a few outsiders, such as mystics and theosophists (in the old sense of the word), could integrate this "secret wisdom" (Walter Nigg). The post-Reformation mystic Jakob Böhme, who in this respect was to become for many a very important stimulating personality, speaks of the divine Sophia: "Before heaven and earth were created, she was a maiden, quite pure and spotless. And this same pure and chaste virgin of God came into Mary when she became flesh and was her new person in the holy element of God." In the Roman Church the last hundred years are reckoned to be the "Marian era." In 1950 the zenith of the Marian era was reached. Pope Pius XII proclaimed on November 1 of that year the dogma of the bodily Assumption of Mary to the applause of half a million believers in front of St. Peter's Basilica in Rome.

Jung saw in this doctrine an uncommonly important sign of the times,[183] because it fulfilled the Old Testament prophecy of a God to be born of the Virgin Mary and the New Testament vision as told by John in the Apocalypse. In this context the psychologist points to the parallelism between the biblical image pointing to the future of the "Marriage of the Lamb" and the classical expression for man's growing to wholeness in the individuation process. A corresponding need of the human psyche for this wholeness is revealed symptomatically in the frequent appearances of Mary during the last decades. "The religious need longs for wholeness, and therefore lays hold of the images of wholeness offered by the unconscious, which, independently of the conscious mind, rise up from the depths of our psychic nature."[184] Seen from this angle, the historical-critical arguments cannot do justice to the dogma. On the other hand, Jung thinks it true to say of this, which he holds to be "the most important religious event since the Reformation," that "the method which the Pope uses in order to demonstrate the truth of the dogma makes sense to the psychological mind, because it bases itself firstly on the necessary prefigurations and secondly on a tradition of religious assertions reaching

148

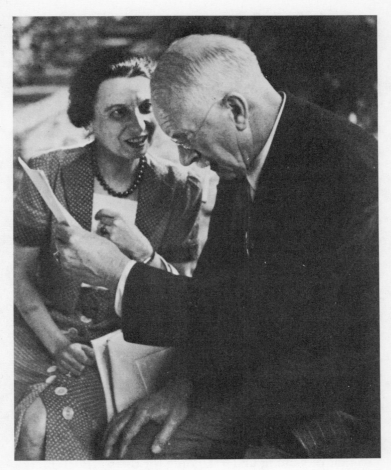

Talking to Jolande Jacobi, about 1948.

back for more than a thousand years. Clearly, the material evidence for the existence of this psychic phenomenon is more than sufficient.'' And he replies as follows to the objection that the new dogma represents a fact which is physically impossible and incapable of proof: ''All re-ligious assertions are physical impossibilities. If they were not so, they would necessarily be treated in the text books of natural science. But religious statements without exception have to do with the reality of the psyche and not with the reality of physics."[185]

Apart from whether the Church dogmatist welcomes the unsolicited agreement of the psychologist or not, Jung's criticism of a Protestant attitude of mind which is patriarchal in nature needs to be considered particularly in respect to man as individuality standing above differentiation by species. Jung adds the following: "Protestantism has obviously not given sufficient attention to the signs of the times which point to the equality of women. But this equality needs to be metaphysically anchored in the figure of a "divine" woman, the bride of Christ. Just as the person of Christ cannot be replaced by an organization"—Jung refers here to the opposite of the "Holy Spirit" thought of as feminine in antiquity and to the organized institutional Church which regulates enthusiasm—"so the bride cannot be replaced by the Church. The feminine, like the masculine, demands an equally personal representation."[186]

The challenge contained in these words—and it concerns the whole book *Answer to Job*—can hardly be ignored. Bound up with it is the question of a renewal of the human image appropriate to contemporary thinking and also that of gaining understanding for the spiritual dimension of the Christian tradition at the present. Jung always saw clearly that others would have to work at the problems which he had brought out into the open. That is why he wrote to his disciple Jolande Jacobi in a letter dated September 24, 1948: "A systematic elaboration of my ideas which are often only sketchy is a task for all who follow me, and without this work there will be no progress in analytical psychology."[187]

THE IMPORTANCE OF DIALOGUE

One can scarcely fail to notice Jung's fundamental attitude to psychic research. Even if one could ignore the type which he convincingly embodies according to his own psychological typology, one must inevitably be struck by the great weight Jung, the "introvert," attaches to the human psyche as a being calling for research into its own nature and its growth. In his view, the human psyche is a complete whole; psychotherapeutic treatment aims at creating this whole. It is not only the drama of life at its essential moments that is played out inside man; he can actually establish a relationship to the inner-psychic complexity and totality which he has been endowed with. Hence—according to Hans Trüb—the "goal is decidedly introspective." This is no denial of the necessity of interhuman relationships, but obviously pays them relatively less attention.

What this means becomes clear if one compares C. G. Jung's nature and work with that of a man for whom the role of dialogue between human beings is so decisive, namely with the German-Jewish philosopher and social thinker Martin Buber. If for Jung everything can be reduced to the common denominator of "experience," to an "id" which calls for research and cure, Martin Buber's life work, at any rate his mature work, is characterized by the relationship between "I and thou." Both thinkers represent basic attitudes, each with a strong emphasis. The positions of Jung and Buber could also be compared to the two foci of an ellipse. Buber himself distinguishes the "I-thou relationship" from the "I-id relationship."

Had both seen the possibility that their attitudes might

be complementary? At any rate, a conversation was begun between Buber and Jung, although it could not be completed. It is all the more significant that there are some Jungians who have understood Buber's request and have pointed out—for themselves to begin with—ways to a synthesis. One of them, Hans Trüb, has shown in his posthumous work *Heilung aus der Begegnung* to what extent he is indebted to both the psychologist Jung and the philosopher Buber. Trüb emphasizes that a purely psychological enrichment, which the inquiring ego experiences by penetrating the unconscious psychic event, is not enough; "eye to eye," as the expression of a confrontation of partners, is required. Of course, Trüb does

Draft in the author's own handwriting for the text of *Psychologischen Typen* (first edition, 1921).

Prof. Dr. C. G. Jung

Küsnacht-Zürich
Seestrasse 228

not overlook, any more than does the disciple of Jung and Buber Arie Sborowitz (*Beziehung und Bestimmung*), that Jung, in comparison with Sigmund Freud, had already taken an important step in the direction indicated by Buber. This is expressed even in the method of treatment which is given to the patient as a concrete opposite person. Hans Trüb sums up: "It is becoming apparent that the future psychotherapist will not be able to concentrate his scientific and therapeutic interest exclusively on complex inner processes and diagnosis as did our pioneers for good reasons and in exemplary fashion. For today we experience and recognize the 'reality of the soul' no longer just as a separate realm of the individual; rather, it reveals itself to us with ever-increasing force as a phenomenon existing between persons within the framework of a life lived in partnership. Only here, in concrete situations of coming together where the world is encountered as creation and history, can the human soul open itself in its true depth of being and reveal itself and the center of its mysterious activity."[188]

This observation could of course be made with equal justification by Jung in regard to a position determined in a one-sided personalistic way; since the need for an I-thou relationship cannot exclude the obligation to know the reality within the soul. Now, whereas Martin Buber—for example, in his book *The Eclipse of God* (1952/53)—wants "reality of faith" to be distinguished from the philosopher's "truth of thought," because the believer cannot make "unconditioned essence" into the object of a mere intellectual search for experience, Jung expresses once again his old position in his *Answer to Buber* (printed in the appendix to the eleventh volume of the *Collected Works*). As an investigator whose only means of cognition is experience, Jung emphasizes: "The 'reality of the soul' is

153

Martin Buber.

the hypothesis with which I work and my main activity
consists in collecting factual material and describing and
explaining it. I have neither worked out a system nor a
general theory but only postulated concepts which serve as
tools, as is usual in any science . . . If I happen to take the
view that all pronouncements about God come in the first
place from the soul and must therefore be distinguished
from the metaphysical being, that is neither to deny God

nor to set man in place of God.''[189] In the same context, Jung recognizes that knowledge of faith can be much more complete ''than we can ever achieve with our laborious and short-winded empiricism.''[190] The psychologist and psychiatrist refrain, however, from making pronouncements going beyond the scientist's field of competence. Jung knew too well that in the realm of faith ''there exist pneumatic structures of extreme beauty and wonderful meaning''; he confesses at the same time that he lacks the necessary charisma of faith for gaining complete access to the pneumatic. It does the psychiatrist credit that he has declared this intimate personal fact so quietly. The conversation between depth psychology and theology to which Jung has important and enriching contributions to offer, can only gain in clarity of concept from that.

In the last years of his life, Jung seems to have realized more and more clearly the importance of the role of dialogue, of the patient facing the doctor, when he says: ''The crucial point is that I confront the patient as one human being to another. Analysis is a dialogue demanding two partners. Analyst and patient sit facing one another, eye to eye; the doctor has something to say, but so has the patient.''[191] And further on: ''As a doctor I constantly have to ask myself what kind of message the patient is bringing me. What does he mean to me? If he means nothing, I have no point of attack. The doctor is effective only when he himself is affected.''[192]

That the dialogue component is especially noticeable and significant in Jung's later work is reflected most forcibly in *Psychology of Transference* (1946), in which we are told how the real person is born essentially from the psychic relationship. Anyone who has followed Jung's way of individuation will be best able to confirm the truth of the following sentences: ''But the conscious achievement

155

of inner unity clings desperately to human relationships as to an indispensable condition, for without the conscious acknowledgement and acceptance of our kinship with those around us there can be no synthesis of personality . . . Because relationship to the self is at once relationship to our fellow man, and no one can be related to the latter until he is related to himself . . . Individuation has two principal aspects; in the first place it is an internal and subjective process of integration, and in the second it is an equally indispensable process of objective relationship. Neither can exist without the other, although sometimes the one and sometimes the other predominates."[193] What sense is there then in the remark that Jung is primarily a man of ego-id experience, and that the I-thou relationship with its dialogue aspect (in the sense of Martin Buber) is of secondary importance to him? It is to the credit of the intellectual profile of a thinker and empiricist like Jung that his work corresponds with the equally strong profile of a communicative thinker such as Martin Buber. Both attitudes should therefore be regarded and appreciated not as alternatives but as complementary. They complete one another even when they are in open or seeming contradiction.

THE REPLY TO JUNG

Even if Sigmund Freud must be credited with the Copernican feat in the field of modern psychology, C. G. Jung has earned for himself an undisputed distinction which puts him in the front rank of the great men of the twentieth century, i.e., by his discovery and investigation of the collective unconscious, the world of the archetypes. The results of his work not only enable one to look into the depth and breadth of the human psyche, not only help to bridge the intellectual polarity of East and West or the gap between past and present, but offer important stimuli in various other fields of learning. If Jung is one day studied as a figure in the intellectual history of Central Europe, possibly in a series of monographs (this important task has yet to be undertaken) not only will the colleague, the disciple, the doctor, the psychologist, the psychiatrist, and the psychotherapist have to make a contribution, but members of a number of other disciplines will have to take part in the reassessment.

The historian in his work on religion or ideas in general, the investigator of symbols and myths, would have to acknowledge the value of Jung's work which has shed further light on these subjects. That such an exchange of experiences did actually take place here long ago is shown by his collaboration with the Sinologist Richard Wilhelm (*The Golden Flower*). Jung has also written commentaries on the Tibetan *Book of the Dead* (1953) and the Tibetan *Book of the Great Liberation* (1955). He collaborated with Karl Kerényi in the literary field, editing with him *An Introduction to the Nature of Mythology. Der göttliche Schelm* (The Godly Rogue), text and comments on the myth of the Winnebago Indians, was completed with the assistance of Kerényi and Paul Radin. It is significant that, after the death of Jung, Kerényi called the first volume of his own works *Humanistische Seelenforschung* (Munich, 1966), thereby indicating the object of his labors in working with Jung. In the circle of that large group of distinguished international collaborators which has met in Ascona since 1933 under the auspices of Olga Fröbe-Kapteyn to take part in the annual Erano conferences, Jung met many people with something to say. The same applies—with a difference in detail—to the annual conferences of the Stuttgart study group "Doctor and Pastor," whose transactions have for many years been carefully recorded by Wilhelm Bitter. Quite apart from the subjects discussed in these contexts which deal partly with research in Jung's special fields, lectures given there would be unthinkable without Jung's pioneering work. Mention must be made here of the Nobel Prize winner W. Paul, with whom Jung worked on problems in science and the theory of cognition as it related to physics and depth psychology. Beyond the circle of disciples in the real sense, there is also the C. G. Jung Institute, founded in Zurich in 1948, which continues and elaborates his work. Its literary output can be found in the series of books *Studies by the C. G. Jung Institute, Zurich.*

The list of those who exchanged views with Jung would be incomplete if the theologians were to be forgotten. True, the dialogue between theology and depth psychol-

Jung's house in Küsnacht.

ogy—if one considers the significance of the insights of depth psychology for the religious life—has only just begun. All the same, Jung has stimulated Protestant, Catholic, and Greek Orthodox theologians. The Protestant theologian Walter Bernet (in H. J. Schultz, *Tendenzen der Theologie im 20 Jahrhundert*, Stuttgart, 1966) ranks Jung among those who have had a decisive influence on contemporaries on Christian theology. For some years the demand has been heard in theological quarters that the lines of thought opened up by Jung should be used more systematically than hitherto. What is remarkable is that this recommendation is occasionally made not only for the practical pastoral work of the minister, where psychological training could be required as an obvious necessity, but also in regard to dogmatic pronouncements. In 1946 Hans Schär wrote in his fine monograph *Religion and the Cure of Souls in Jung's Psychology:* "Theologians have not examined Jung's results to the extent that really might be expected in view of the facts."[194] Today the willingness on the part of the theologians to make some contact seems to be steadily increasing.

The philosopher too has his part to play in these conversations with representatives of Jungian psychology. For instance, there was some justification for their criticism of the method of amplification which, they said, was based exclusively on conclusions by analogy. An examination based on the theory of cognition would be profitable, and, indeed, not only for Jung's method of working and its assumptions. On the other hand, the results of depth psychology itself seriously question the validity of the intellectual horizon of present-day science. What is involved here is the question whether and with what right statements can be made about exact knowledge of the spiritual world which transcends the traditional concept of

159

science. Jung did of course deliberately confine himself to increasing our knowledge of the psyche, but the results obtained absolutely demand an up-to-date investigation into the supernatural world of the spirit. Hans Erhard Lauer is one of the few who, together with the disciple of Jung Alice Morawitz-Cadio, has supplied the first contribution to this and attempted to build a bridge between depth psychology and modern knowledge of the spirit. This beginning needs to be continued and extended. Scholastic and dogmatic tendencies to become entrenched, which—as is only too well known—plague any intellectual movement, should be resisted.

Psychology, more than most other sciences, is able to fulfill the function of building bridges between other disciplines. The extent to which opinions can be reconciled and how far the particular results obtained in one field can be put to good use in another will depend on the willingness of its practitioners. In his work Jung has supplied a wealth of examples. Of course, we cannot overlook the fact that he had to defend himself against many critics who did not always succeed in understanding his intentions. He complained once that "it is certainly remarkable that my critics, with few exceptions, ignore the fact that, as a doctor, I proceed from facts which everyone is at liberty to verify. Instead, they criticize me as if I were a philosopher, or a Gnostic with pretensions to supernatural knowledge. As a philosopher and speculating heretic I am, of course, easy prey. That is probably the reason why people prefer to ignore the facts I have discovered."[195]

Finally, the extent to which Carl Gustav Jung gave everything he had and called for a response is made manifest in the numerous honors which came from all parts of the world. On his sixtieth birthday, disciples and

1960.

friends expressed their recognition in a publication entitled *The Cultural Significance of Complex Psychology*. The
famous Eranos yearbooks produced a volume of *Studies for
C. G. Jung* for his seventieth and again for his seventy-fifth
birthday. Two further important volumes of essays were
issued by the C. G. Jung Institute, Zurich, on the occasion
of his eightieth birthday. Together with the numerous and
steadily increasing *Studies of the C. G. Jung Institute*, they
document the way in which analytical psychology has
opened our eyes to reality. Carl Gustav Jung was a
member of numerous scholarly societies in Switzerland
and throughout the world. The Royal Society of Medicine, London, made him an honorary member.
The following universities conferred an honorary

doctorate on him: Clark University, Fordham University, Harvard University, Hindu University, University of Allahabad, University of Calcutta, Oxford University, University of Geneva, Eidgenössische Technische Hochschule, Zurich.

Who the recipient of all this recognition and all these honors was, is precisely and concisely stated in the document recording the award of the honorary doctorate of the Eidgenössische Technische Hochschule:

"To the man who rediscovered the wholeness and polarity of the human psyche and its tendency to integration;

"To the diagnostician of the symptoms of crisis in the human race in the age of science and technology;

"To the interpreter of primal symbolism and the process of individuation in mankind."[196]

Carl Jung died in 1961, at the age of eighty-five.

NOTES

1. Georg Gerster, *Eine Stunde mit C. G. Jung* (Frankfurt, 1956), p. 18.
2. C. G. Jung, *Memories, Dreams Reflections*, trans. R. and C. Winston (New York and London, 1963), p. 18
3. *Errinnerungen, Träume, Gedanken* (Zurich, 1963), p. 11.
4. *Memories, Dreams, Reflections*, p. 21.
5. *Ibid.*, p. 18.
6. *Ibid.*, p. 25.
7. *Ibid.*, p. 28.
8. *Ibid.*, p. 55.
9. *Ibid.*, p. 58.
10. *Ibid.*, p. 70.
11. *Ibid.*, p. 52.
12. *Ibid.*, p. 56.
13. *Ibid.*, p. 37.
14. *Ibid.*, p. 76.
15. *Ibid.*, p. 77.
16. *Ibid.*, p. 78.
17. *Ibid.*
18. *Ibid.*, p. 82.
19. *Ibid.*, p. 101.
20. *Ibid.*, p. 103. As the well-known parapsychologist Dr. Gerda Walther suggested to me (December 1968), the reports of the Swabian theologian Johann Christoph Blumhardt (1805-1880) about his experiences in Möttlingen must have had a lasting influence on Jung as a student.
21. *Ibid.*, p. 110.
22. E. A. Bennett, *C. G. Jung* (London and New York, 1961), p. 147.
23. *Memories, Dreams, Reflections*, p. 143.
24. *Works*, vol. 3, trans. R. F. C. Hull (New York and London, 1960), p. 3.
25. *Works*, vol. 7, (1953), p. 9.
26. *Memories, Dreams, Reflections*, p. 146.
27. *Ibid.*, p. 147.
28. *Ibid*, p. 146.
29. *Ibid.*, p. 148.
30. *Ibid.*
31. *Ibid.*, p. 152.
32. *Ibid.*
33. *Ibid.*, p. 154.
34. *Ibid.*, p. 162.
35. *Ibid.*
36. *Ibid.*
37. *Ibid.*, p. 144.
38. *Ibid.*, p. 163

39. Foreword to Jolande Jacobi, *Die Psychologie von C. G. Jung* (Zurich, 1945), p. 18. This Foreword, dating from 1939, is important for an understanding of Jung.

40. *Werke,* vol. 11 (Zurich), p. 660.

41. *Ibid.,* p. 658.

42. *Wirklichkeit der Seele* (Zurich, 1939), p. 24.

43. *Memories, Dreams, Reflections,* p. 323.

44. *Works,* vol. 8 (1960), p. 185.

45. *Ibid.,* p. 4.

46. *Ibid.,* p. 17.

47. C. G. Jung, *Von den Wurzeln des Bewusstseins* (Zurich, 1954), p. 4.

48. *Ibid.,* p. 6, and also p. 577.

49. *Symbolik des Geistes* (Zurich, 1953), p. 374.

50. *Werke,* vol. 6, pp. 512 ff.

51. *Works,* vol. 7, p. 171.

52. *Von den Wurzeln des Bewusstseins,* p. 591.

53. *Werke,* vol. 6, p. 477.

54. *Von den Wurzeln des Bewusstseins,* pp. 53 ff.

55. Jolande Jacobi, *The Psychology of Jung* (London and New York, fifth edition, 1951), p. 42.

56. *Memories, Dreams, Reflections,* p. 239.

57. *Works,* vol. 11, p. 197.

58. *Ibid.,* vol. 8, p. 55.

59. *Ibid.,* vol. 11, p. 169.

60. Riwkah Schärf, in *Symbolik des Geistes,* pp. 153-319.

61. *Works,* vol. 11, p. 45.

62. *Memories, Dreams, Reflections,* p. 349.

63. *Works,* vol. 7, p. 190.

64. *Ibid.,* p. 290.

65. *Memories, Dreams, Reflections,* p. 184.

66. *Werke,* vol. 6, p. xi.

67. *Works,* vol. 7., p. 43.

68. *Memories, Dreams, Reflections,* p. 352.

69. C. G. Jung, *Psychological Types* (New York and London, 1923), p. 547.

70. *Ibid.,* p. 613.

71. *Ibid.,* p. 55.

72. *Ibid.,* p. 511.

73. *Ibid.,* p. 512.

74. *Memories, Dreams, Reflections,* p. 198.

75. *Works,* vol. 7. p. 40.

76. *Ibid.,* p. 42.

77. Quotation from Bennett, p. 82.

78. *Works,* vol. 16, p. 5.

79. *Memories, Dreams, Reflections,* p. 70.

80. *Ibid.*

81. *Works,* vol. 11, p. 3.

82. *Ibid.,* p. 1.

83. Hans Schär. *Religion and the Cure of Souls in the Psychology of C. G. Jung* (London, 1951).

84. Wilhelm Bitter, *Psychotherapie und religiöse Erfahrung* (Stuttgart, 1965), p. 79.

85. *Works,* vol. 11, p. 8.

86. *Ibid.*, vol. 12, p. 9.
87. *Ibid.*, p. 10.
88. *Ibid.*
89. *Ibid.*, p. 11.
90. *Ibid.*
91. *Von den Wurzeln des Bewusstseins*, p. 72.
92. *Works*, vol. 11, p. 58.
93. *Ibid.*, pp. 58-59.
94. *Ibid.*, vol. 12, p. 7.
95. *Ibid.*, p. 12.
96. *Ibid.*
97. *Ibid.*, p. 17.
98. *Ibid.*, vol. 9, Part 2, p. 69.
99. *Ibid.*, vol. 8, p. 276.
100. *Ibid.*, vol. 11, p. 441.
101. *Symbolik des Geistes*, pp. 381, 384.
102. Schär, p. 273.
103. *Memories, Dreams, Reflections*, p. 192.
104. Cf. among others Gerhard Wehr, *Auf den Spuren unchristlicher Ketzer*, vols. 1-11 (Freiburg, 1965-1967).
105. *Memories, Dreams, Reflections*, p. 192.
106. *Ibid.*, pp. 192-193.
107. *Ibid.*, p. 193.
108. *Werke*, vol. 13, p. 55.
109. *Memories, Dreams, Reflections*, p. 200.
110. *Werke*, vol. 12, p. 99.
111. *Ibid.*, p. 228.
112. *Ibid.*, p. 245.
113. *Memories, Dreams, Reflections*, p. 209.
114. Rudolf Steiner, *Tension between East and West* (London, 1963).
115. *Werke*, vol. 11, p. 531.
116. *Works*, vol. 11, p. 4.
117. *Ibid.*
118. *Das Geheimnis der Goldenen Blüte* (Zurich, 1965), p. xii.
119. *Ibid.*, p. xvii.
120. *Ibid.*
121. *Werke*, vol. 11, p. 574.
122. *Ibid.*, p. 576.
123. *Ibid.*, p. 575.
124. *Ibid.*, p. 576.
125. *Ibid.*, p. 580.
126. *Ibid.*
127. *Ibid.*, pp. 576 ff.
128. *Ibid.*, p. 577.
129. *Memories, Dreams, Reflections*, p. 232.
130. *Ibid.*, p. 239.
131. *Ibid.*, p. 257.
132. *Works*, vol. 11, p. 577.
133. *Ibid.*
134. *Erinnerungen, Träume, Gedanken*, p. 279.
135. *Memories, Dreams, Reflections*, p. 257.
136. *Ibid.*

137. *Ibid.*, p. 264.
138. *Das Geheimnis der Goldenen Blüte*, p. xiii.
139. *Ibid.*, p. xiv.
140. *Works*, vol. 8, p. 518.
141. *Ibid.*, p. 519.
142. *Werke*, vol. 16, p. ix.
143. *Ibid.*, pp. 130 ff.
144. *Ibid.*, p. 38.
145. *Works*, vol. 16, p. 3.
146. *Ibid.*, p. 8.
147. *Memories, Dreams, Reflections*, p. 132.
148. *Ibid.*, p. 130.
149. *Werke*, vol. 16, p. 111.
150. *Ibid.*, p. 115.
151. *Works*, vol. 16, p. 81.
152. *Ibid.*, p. 23.
153. *Ibid.*, p. 31.
154. *Ibid.*
155. S. Freud, *Outline of Psychoanalysis* (London, 1949), p. 26.
156. *Werke*, vol. 11, p. 27.
157. *Seelenprobleme der Gegenwart* (Zurich, 1931), p. 98.
158. *Works*, vol. 11, p. 26.
159. *Ibid.*, vol. 8, p. 237.
160. *Ibid.*, vol. 11, p. 27.
161. *Ibid.*, vol. 7, p. 99.
162. *Ibid.*, vol. 8, p. 243.
163. *Psychological Types*, p. 108.
164. *Works*, vol. 8, p. 240.
165. *Ibid.*, p. 250.
166. *Ibid.*, p. 266.
167. *Ibid.*, p. 267.
168. *Ibid.*, vol. 11, p. 306.
169. Jacobi, *The Psychology of Jung*, p. 112.
170. *Essays on Contemporary Events* (London, 1947), p. vii.
171. *Ibid.*, p. 76.
172. *Ibid.*, p. 4.
173. *Ibid.*, p. 10.
174. *Ibid.*, p. 15.
175. *Ibid.*, p. 16.
176. *Ibid.*
177. Aniela Jaffé, *Aus Leben und Werkstatt von C. G. Jung* (Zurich, 1968), pp. 85-104.
178. *Ein moderner Mythus* (Zurich, 1964), p. 105.
179. *Works*, vol. 11, p. 365.
180. *Ibid.*, p. 377.
181. *Ibid.*, p. 405.
182. *Werke*, vol. 11, p. 506.
183. *Works*, vol. 11, p. 458.
184. *Ibid.*, p. 469.
185. *Ibid.*, p. 464.
186. *Ibid.*, p. 465.
187. Jolande Jacobi, *Der Weg zur Individuation* (Zurich, 1965), p. 7.

188. Hans Trüb, *Heilung aus der Begegnung* (Stuttgart, 1962), pp. 15 ff.
189. *Werke,* vol. 11, p. 660.
190. *Ibid.,* p. 663.
191. *Memories, Dreams, Reflections,* p. 131.
192. *Ibid.,* p. 133.
193. *Works,* vol. 16, pp. 247 ff.
194. Schär, *Religion und Seele in der Psychologie von C. G. Jung* (Zurich, 1946), p. 10.
195. *Works,* vol. 11, p. 307.
196. *Zum 85. Geburtstag . . .* (Zurich, 1960), p. 3.

Chronology

<table>
<tr><td>1875</td><td>Born on July 26th in Kesswil, canton of Thurgau; the son of the parson, Johann Paul Achilles Jung (1842–1896) and his wife Emilie, née Preiswerk (1848–1923).</td></tr>
<tr><td>1879</td><td>The family moves to Klein-Hüningen near Basle. Attends the Gymnasium in Basle.</td></tr>
<tr><td>1895–1900</td><td>Studies medicine in Basle; takes state examination. Second assistant at the Burghölzli Psychiatric Clinic of the University of Zurich. Dissertation: On the Psychology and Pathology of Supposed Occult Phenomena.</td></tr>
<tr><td>1902–1903</td><td>Spends the winter term under Janet in Paris.</td></tr>
<tr><td>1903</td><td>Marriage to Emma Rauschenbach, Schaffhausen.</td></tr>
<tr><td>1903–1905</td><td>Assistant physician at the Psychiatric Clinic in Zurich.</td></tr>
<tr><td>1905–1909</td><td>Senior physician at the clinic.</td></tr>
<tr><td>1905–1913</td><td>Lecturer in the Medical Faculty of the University of Zurich; lectures on psychoneurosis and psychology.</td></tr>
<tr><td>1906</td><td>Studies the work of Sigmund Freud.</td></tr>
<tr><td>1907</td><td>February, first meeting with Freud in Vienna. The Psychology of Dementia Praecox.</td></tr>
<tr><td>1909</td><td>Resignation of post at clinic; private practice in Küsnacht/Zurich; lectures on the association method at Clark University; editor of the</td></tr>
</table>

Jahrbuch für psychologische und psychopatho-logische Forschungen, edited by Freud and Bleuler.

1911　Foundation of the Internationale Psychoana-lytische Gesellschaft; Jung the first president.

1912　*Transformations and Symbols of the Libido;* lec-tures on psychoanalytical theory at Fordham University.

1912–1913　Breaks away from the psychoanalytical move-ment of Freud; Jung calls his own research work "Analytical Psychology."

1914　Lectures in London and Aberdeen; captain in the army medical service working in intern-ment camps.

1916　*Die transzendente Funktion; The Psychology of the Unconscious.*

1921　*Pyschological Types.* Journey to North Africa.

1924–1925　Field study of the Pueblo Indians in Arizona and New Mexico.

1925–1926　Field study of the Elgonyis on Mount Elgon, East Africa.

1928　*The Relations between the Ego and the Uncon-scious; On Psychic Energy.*

1930　Honorary President of the Deutsche Ärzt-liche Gesellschaft für Psychotherapie.

1931　*The Spiritual Problem of Opposites.*

1932　Literary Prize of the City of Zurich.

1933　President of the Internationale Allgemeine Ärztliche Gesellschaft für Psychotherapie; resumed academic lectures at the Eidgenös-sische Technische Hochschule in Zurich; edi-tor of the *Zentralblatt für Psychotherapie und ihre Grenzgebiete.*

1934	*The Reality of the Soul.*
1935	Publication marking his sixtieth birthday: *The Cultural Significance of Complex Psychology.* Appointed titular professor.
1937	Trip to India. Lectures at Yale University (Terry Lectures: *Psychology and Religion*).
1940	Publication of *Psychology and Religion.*
1942	*Paraclesica;* with Karl Kerényi, *Essays on a Science of Mythology.*
1944	*Psychology and Alchemy.* Appointment as Professor of Medical Psychology at the University of Basle.
1946	*Psychology and Education; Essays on Contemporary Events; Psychology of Transference.* Inauguration of the C. G. Jung Institute in Zurich. *Symbols of the Mind.*
1951	*Aion.*
1952	*Symbols of Transformation; Answer to Job; Synchronicity as a Universal Acausal Principle.*
1954	*On the Origins of Consciousness.*
1955	*Mysterium Coniunctionis;* publication to mark his eightieth birthday: *Studies on the Analytical Psychology of C. G. Jung.* Wife dies on November 27th. *The Future of Opposites.*
1958	*A Modern Myth.*
1960	Nominated Freeman of Küsnacht/Zurich on the occasion of his eighty-fifth birthday.
1961	*Approaching the Unconscious,* his last book, published, at first only in English. Dies on June 6th in Küsnacht.

BIBLIOGRAPHY

Works

Aion: Researches into the Phenomenology of the Self. In *Collected Works*, Vol. 9, Part 2. Princeton, second edition, 1968.

Alchemical Studies. In *Collected Works*, Vol. 13. Princeton, 1968.

Analytical Psychology, Its Theory and Practice: The Tavistock Lectures, 1935. New York, 1968.

Answer to Job. New York (paper edition).

Archetypes and the Collective Unconscious. In *Collected Works*, Vol. 9, Part 1. Princeton, second edition, 1969.

Basic Writings of C. G. Jung. New York, 1959.

Civilization in Transition. In *Collected Works*, Vol. 10. Princeton, 1964.

Development of Personality. In *Collected Works*, Vol. 17. Princeton, 1954.

Experimental Researches. In *Collected Works*, Vol. 2. Princeton.

Flying Saucers: A Modern Myth of Things Seen in the Skies. New York, 1969.

Freud and Psychoanalysis. In *Collected Works*, Vol. 4. Princeton, 1961.

Man and His Symbols. New York, 1968.

Memories, Dreams, Reflections. New York, 1963.

Modern Man in Search of a Soul. New York.

On the Nature of the Psyche. Princeton (paper edition).

Practice of Psychotherapy. In *Collected Works*, Vol. 16. Princeton, 1966.

Psyche and Symbol: A Selection from the Writings of C. G. Jung. New York, 1958.

Psychiatric Studies. In *Collected Works,* Vol. 1. Princeton, 1957.

Psychogenesis of Mental Disease. In *Collected Works,* Vol. 3. Princeton, 1960.

Psychological Reflections. Princeton, 1953.

Psychology and Education. Princeton (paper edition).

Psychology and Religion: West and East. In *Collected Works,* Vol. 11. Princeton, second edition, 1969.

Psychology of the Transference. Princeton (paper edition).

The Spirit in Man, Art and Literature. In *Collected Works,* Vol. 15. Princeton, 1966.

The Structure and Dynamics of the Psyche. In *Collected Works,* Vol. 12. Princeton, 1969.

Symbols of Transformation. In *Collected Works,* Vol. 5. Princeton, second edition, 1967.

Two Essays on Analytical Psychology. In *Collected Works,* Vol. 7. Princeton, second edition, 1966.

Undiscovered Self. New York, 1959.

Jung et al. *Studies in Word Association.* New York, 1969.

Jung, and Carl Kerényi. *Essays on a Science of Mythology.* Princeton, revised edition, 1963.

Jung, and W. Pauli. *Interpretation of Nature and the Psyche.* Princeton, 1955.

Wilhelm, Richard, and C. G. Jung. *Secret of the Golden Flower.* New York, revised edition, 1962.

Works about Jung and His Psychology

BENNETT, E. A. *C. G. Jung.* New York (paper edition).
———. *What Jung Really Said.* New York, 1967.
BERTINE, ELEANOR. *Jung's Contribution to Our Time: The Collected Papers of Eleanor Bertine.* New York, 1968.

CLARK, ROBERT. *Six Talks on Jung's Psychology*. Pittsburgh, 1953.

COX, DAVID. *Modern Psychology: The Teachings of Carl Gustav Jung*. New York, 1968.

DRY, AVIS M. *The Psychology of Jung*. New York, 1961.

FORDHAM, FRIEDA. *Introduction to Jung's Psychology*. New York (paper edition).

FORDHAM, MICHAEL. *Contact with Jung*. New York, 1963.

_____. *New Developments in Analytical Psychology*. New York.

GLOVER, EDWARD. *Freud or Jung?* New York, 1956.

GOLDBRUNNER, JOSEF. *Individuation: A Study of the Depth Psychology of Carl Gustav Jung*. Notre Dame, Ind., 1964.

HANNA, CHARLES B. *Face of the Deep: The Religious Ideas of C. G. Jung*. Philadelphia, 1967.

HOCHHEIMER, WOLFGANG. *Psychotherapy of C. G. Jung*. New York, 1969.

JACOBI, JOLANDE. *Complex Archetype Symbol in the Psychology of C. G. Jung*. Princeton, 1959.

_____. *Psychology of C. G. Jung*. New Haven, revised edition, 1963.

_____. *Way of Individuation*. New York, 1967.

MAHONEY, MARIA F. *Meaning in Dreams and Dreaming*. New York, 1966.

MARTIN, P. W. *Experiment in Depth: A Study of Jung, Eliot and Toynbee*. New York.

MORENO, A. *Jung, Gods, and Modern Man*. Notre Dame, Ind., 1970.

PHILIPSON, MORRIS. *Outline of Jungian Aesthetics*. Chicago, 1963.

PROGOFF, IRA. *Jung's Psychology and Its Social Meaning*. New York, revised edition, 1969.

SERRANO, MIGUEL. *C. G. Jung and Hermann Hesse: A Record of Two Friendships*. New York, 1966.

WHITE, VICTOR. *God and the Unconscious*. New York, 1961.